T0243405

THIS IS YOUR **PASSBOOK®** FOR ...

OFFICE ASSISTANT

NLC®

NATIONAL LEARNING CORPORATION®
passbooks.com

COPYRIGHT NOTICE

Copyright © 2021 by

NLC®

National Learning Corporation

212 Michael Drive, Syosset, NY 11791
(516) 921-8888 • www.passbooks.com
E-mail: info@passbooks.com

PUBLISHED IN THE UNITED STATES OF AMERICA

PASSBOOK® SERIES

THE *PASSBOOK® SERIES* has been created to prepare applicants and candidates for the ultimate academic battlefield – the examination room.

At some time in our lives, each and every one of us may be required to take an examination – for validation, matriculation, admission, qualification, registration, certification, or licensure.

Based on the assumption that every applicant or candidate has met the basic formal educational standards, has taken the required number of courses, and read the necessary texts, the *PASSBOOK® SERIES* furnishes the one special preparation which may assure passing with confidence, instead of failing with insecurity. Examination questions – together with answers – are furnished as the basic vehicle for study so that the mysteries of the examination and its compounding difficulties may be eliminated or diminished by a sure method.

This book is meant to help you pass your examination provided that you qualify and are serious in your objective.

The entire field is reviewed through the huge store of content information which is succinctly presented through a provocative and challenging approach – the question-and-answer method.

A climate of success is established by furnishing the correct answers at the end of each test.

You soon learn to recognize types of questions, forms of questions, and patterns of questioning. You may even begin to anticipate expected outcomes.

You perceive that many questions are repeated or adapted so that you can gain acute insights, which may enable you to score many sure points.

You learn how to confront new questions, or types of questions, and to attack them confidently and work out the correct answers.

You note objectives and emphases, and recognize pitfalls and dangers, so that you may make positive educational adjustments.

Moreover, you are kept fully informed in relation to new concepts, methods, practices, and directions in the field.

You discover that you arre actually taking the examination all the time: you are preparing for the examination by "taking" an examination, not by reading extraneous and/or supererogatory textbooks.

In short, this PASSBOOK®, used directedly, should be an important factor in helping you to pass your test.

OFFICE ASSISTANT

DUTIES

Performs various clerical duties, typing, and record keeping for a department. Represents the department to the general public in daily office operations; does related work as required.

SCOPE OF THE EXAMINATION

The multiple-choice written test will cover knowledge, skills, and/or abilities in such areas as:

1. Office practices;
2. Clerical aptitude;
3. Verbal ability;
4. Understanding and interpreting written material; and
5. Arithmetical reasoning.

———

HOW TO TAKE A TEST

I. YOU MUST PASS AN EXAMINATION

A. *WHAT EVERY CANDIDATE SHOULD KNOW*

Examination applicants often ask us for help in preparing for the written test. What can I study in advance? What kinds of questions will be asked? How will the test be given? How will the papers be graded?

As an applicant for a civil service examination, you may be wondering about some of these things. Our purpose here is to suggest effective methods of advance study and to describe civil service examinations.

Your chances for success on this examination can be increased if you know how to prepare. Those "pre-examination jitters" can be reduced if you know what to expect. You can even experience an adventure in good citizenship if you know why civil service exams are given.

B. *WHY ARE CIVIL SERVICE EXAMINATIONS GIVEN?*

Civil service examinations are important to you in two ways. As a citizen, you want public jobs filled by employees who know how to do their work. As a job seeker, you want a fair chance to compete for that job on an equal footing with other candidates. The best-known means of accomplishing this two-fold goal is the competitive examination.

Exams are widely publicized throughout the nation. They may be administered for jobs in federal, state, city, municipal, town or village governments or agencies.

Any citizen may apply, with some limitations, such as the age or residence of applicants. Your experience and education may be reviewed to see whether you meet the requirements for the particular examination. When these requirements exist, they are reasonable and applied consistently to all applicants. Thus, a competitive examination may cause you some uneasiness now, but it is your privilege and safeguard.

C. *HOW ARE CIVIL SERVICE EXAMS DEVELOPED?*

Examinations are carefully written by trained technicians who are specialists in the field known as "psychological measurement," in consultation with recognized authorities in the field of work that the test will cover. These experts recommend the subject matter areas or skills to be tested; only those knowledges or skills important to your success on the job are included. The most reliable books and source materials available are used as references. Together, the experts and technicians judge the difficulty level of the questions.

Test technicians know how to phrase questions so that the problem is clearly stated. Their ethics do not permit "trick" or "catch" questions. Questions may have been tried out on sample groups, or subjected to statistical analysis, to determine their usefulness.

Written tests are often used in combination with performance tests, ratings of training and experience, and oral interviews. All of these measures combine to form the best-known means of finding the right person for the right job.

II. HOW TO PASS THE WRITTEN TEST

A. NATURE OF THE EXAMINATION

To prepare intelligently for civil service examinations, you should know how they differ from school examinations you have taken. In school you were assigned certain definite pages to read or subjects to cover. The examination questions were quite detailed and usually emphasized memory. Civil service exams, on the other hand, try to discover your present ability to perform the duties of a position, plus your potentiality to learn these duties. In other words, a civil service exam attempts to predict how successful you will be. Questions cover such a broad area that they cannot be as minute and detailed as school exam questions.

In the public service similar kinds of work, or positions, are grouped together in one "class." This process is known as *position-classification*. All the positions in a class are paid according to the salary range for that class. One class title covers all of these positions, and they are all tested by the same examination.

B. FOUR BASIC STEPS

1) Study the announcement

How, then, can you know what subjects to study? Our best answer is: "Learn as much as possible about the class of positions for which you've applied." The exam will test the knowledge, skills and abilities needed to do the work.

Your most valuable source of information about the position you want is the official exam announcement. This announcement lists the training and experience qualifications. Check these standards and apply only if you come reasonably close to meeting them.

The brief description of the position in the examination announcement offers some clues to the subjects which will be tested. Think about the job itself. Review the duties in your mind. Can you perform them, or are there some in which you are rusty? Fill in the blank spots in your preparation.

Many jurisdictions preview the written test in the exam announcement by including a section called "Knowledge and Abilities Required," "Scope of the Examination," or some similar heading. Here you will find out specifically what fields will be tested.

2) Review your own background

Once you learn in general what the position is all about, and what you need to know to do the work, ask yourself which subjects you already know fairly well and which need improvement. You may wonder whether to concentrate on improving your strong areas or on building some background in your fields of weakness. When the announcement has specified "some knowledge" or "considerable knowledge," or has used adjectives like "beginning principles of..." or "advanced ... methods," you can get a clue as to the number and difficulty of questions to be asked in any given field. More questions, and hence broader coverage, would be included for those subjects which are more important in the work. Now weigh your strengths and weaknesses against the job requirements and prepare accordingly.

3) Determine the level of the position

Another way to tell how intensively you should prepare is to understand the level of the job for which you are applying. Is it the entering level? In other words, is this the position in which beginners in a field of work are hired? Or is it an intermediate or advanced level? Sometimes this is indicated by such words as "Junior" or "Senior" in the class title. Other jurisdictions use Roman numerals to designate the level – Clerk I, Clerk II, for example. The word "Supervisor" sometimes appears in the title. If the level is not indicated by the title, check the description of duties. Will you be working under very close supervision, or will you have responsibility for independent decisions in this work?

4) Choose appropriate study materials

Now that you know the subjects to be examined and the relative amount of each subject to be covered, you can choose suitable study materials. For beginning level jobs, or even advanced ones, if you have a pronounced weakness in some aspect of your training, read a modern, standard textbook in that field. Be sure it is up to date and has general coverage. Such books are normally available at your library, and the librarian will be glad to help you locate one. For entry-level positions, questions of appropriate difficulty are chosen – neither highly advanced questions, nor those too simple. Such questions require careful thought but not advanced training.

If the position for which you are applying is technical or advanced, you will read more advanced, specialized material. If you are already familiar with the basic principles of your field, elementary textbooks would waste your time. Concentrate on advanced textbooks and technical periodicals. Think through the concepts and review difficult problems in your field.

These are all general sources. You can get more ideas on your own initiative, following these leads. For example, training manuals and publications of the government agency which employs workers in your field can be useful, particularly for technical and professional positions. A letter or visit to the government department involved may result in more specific study suggestions, and certainly will provide you with a more definite idea of the exact nature of the position you are seeking.

III. KINDS OF TESTS

Tests are used for purposes other than measuring knowledge and ability to perform specified duties. For some positions, it is equally important to test ability to make adjustments to new situations or to profit from training. In others, basic mental abilities not dependent on information are essential. Questions which test these things may not appear as pertinent to the duties of the position as those which test for knowledge and information. Yet they are often highly important parts of a fair examination. For very general questions, it is almost impossible to help you direct your study efforts. What we can do is to point out some of the more common of these general abilities needed in public service positions and describe some typical questions.

1) General information

Broad, general information has been found useful for predicting job success in some kinds of work. This is tested in a variety of ways, from vocabulary lists to questions about current events. Basic background in some field of work, such as sociology or economics, may be sampled in a group of questions. Often these are principles which have become familiar to most persons through exposure rather than through formal training. It is difficult to advise you how to study for these questions; being alert to the world around you is our best suggestion.

2) Verbal ability

An example of an ability needed in many positions is verbal or language ability. Verbal ability is, in brief, the ability to use and understand words. Vocabulary and grammar tests are typical measures of this ability. Reading comprehension or paragraph interpretation questions are common in many kinds of civil service tests. You are given a paragraph of written material and asked to find its central meaning.

3) Numerical ability

Number skills can be tested by the familiar arithmetic problem, by checking paired lists of numbers to see which are alike and which are different, or by interpreting charts and graphs. In the latter test, a graph may be printed in the test booklet which you are asked to use as the basis for answering questions.

4) Observation

A popular test for law-enforcement positions is the observation test. A picture is shown to you for several minutes, then taken away. Questions about the picture test your ability to observe both details and larger elements.

5) Following directions

In many positions in the public service, the employee must be able to carry out written instructions dependably and accurately. You may be given a chart with several columns, each column listing a variety of information. The questions require you to carry out directions involving the information given in the chart.

6) Skills and aptitudes

Performance tests effectively measure some manual skills and aptitudes. When the skill is one in which you are trained, such as typing or shorthand, you can practice. These tests are often very much like those given in business school or high school courses. For many of the other skills and aptitudes, however, no short-time preparation can be made. Skills and abilities natural to you or that you have developed throughout your lifetime are being tested.

Many of the general questions just described provide all the data needed to answer the questions and ask you to use your reasoning ability to find the answers. Your best preparation for these tests, as well as for tests of facts and ideas, is to be at your physical and mental best. You, no doubt, have your own methods of getting into an exam-taking mood and keeping "in shape." The next section lists some ideas on this subject.

IV. KINDS OF QUESTIONS

Only rarely is the "essay" question, which you answer in narrative form, used in civil service tests. Civil service tests are usually of the short-answer type. Full instructions for answering these questions will be given to you at the examination. But in case this is your first experience with short-answer questions and separate answer sheets, here is what you need to know:

1) Multiple-choice Questions

Most popular of the short-answer questions is the "multiple choice" or "best answer" question. It can be used, for example, to test for factual knowledge, ability to solve problems or judgment in meeting situations found at work.

A multiple-choice question is normally one of three types—

- It can begin with an incomplete statement followed by several possible endings. You are to find the one ending which *best* completes the statement, although some of the others may not be entirely wrong.
- It can also be a complete statement in the form of a question which is answered by choosing one of the statements listed.
- It can be in the form of a problem – again you select the best answer.

Here is an example of a multiple-choice question with a discussion which should give you some clues as to the method for choosing the right answer:

When an employee has a complaint about his assignment, the action which will *best* help him overcome his difficulty is to
- A. discuss his difficulty with his coworkers
- B. take the problem to the head of the organization
- C. take the problem to the person who gave him the assignment
- D. say nothing to anyone about his complaint

In answering this question, you should study each of the choices to find which is best. Consider choice "A" – Certainly an employee may discuss his complaint with fellow employees, but no change or improvement can result, and the complaint remains unresolved. Choice "B" is a poor choice since the head of the organization probably does not know what assignment you have been given, and taking your problem to him is known as "going over the head" of the supervisor. The supervisor, or person who made the assignment, is the person who can clarify it or correct any injustice. Choice "C" is, therefore, correct. To say nothing, as in choice "D," is unwise. Supervisors have and interest in knowing the problems employees are facing, and the employee is seeking a solution to his problem.

2) True/False Questions

The "true/false" or "right/wrong" form of question is sometimes used. Here a complete statement is given. Your job is to decide whether the statement is right or wrong.

SAMPLE: A roaming cell-phone call to a nearby city costs less than a non-roaming call to a distant city.

This statement is wrong, or false, since roaming calls are more expensive.
This is not a complete list of all possible question forms, although most of the others are variations of these common types. You will always get complete directions for

answering questions. Be sure you understand *how* to mark your answers – ask questions until you do.

V. RECORDING YOUR ANSWERS

Computer terminals are used more and more today for many different kinds of exams.

For an examination with very few applicants, you may be told to record your answers in the test booklet itself. Separate answer sheets are much more common. If this separate answer sheet is to be scored by machine – and this is often the case – it is highly important that you mark your answers correctly in order to get credit.

An electronic scoring machine is often used in civil service offices because of the speed with which papers can be scored. Machine-scored answer sheets must be marked with a pencil, which will be given to you. This pencil has a high graphite content which responds to the electronic scoring machine. As a matter of fact, stray dots may register as answers, so do not let your pencil rest on the answer sheet while you are pondering the correct answer. Also, if your pencil lead breaks or is otherwise defective, ask for another.

Since the answer sheet will be dropped in a slot in the scoring machine, be careful not to bend the corners or get the paper crumpled.

The answer sheet normally has five vertical columns of numbers, with 30 numbers to a column. These numbers correspond to the question numbers in your test booklet. After each number, going across the page are four or five pairs of dotted lines. These short dotted lines have small letters or numbers above them. The first two pairs may also have a "T" or "F" above the letters. This indicates that the first two pairs only are to be used if the questions are of the true-false type. If the questions are multiple choice, disregard the "T" and "F" and pay attention only to the small letters or numbers.

Answer your questions in the manner of the sample that follows:

32. The largest city in the United States is
   A. Washington, D.C.
   B. New York City
   C. Chicago
   D. Detroit
   E. San Francisco

1) Choose the answer you think is best. (New York City is the largest, so "B" is correct.)
2) Find the row of dotted lines numbered the same as the question you are answering. (Find row number 32)
3) Find the pair of dotted lines corresponding to the answer. (Find the pair of lines under the mark "B.")
4) Make a solid black mark between the dotted lines.

VI. BEFORE THE TEST

Common sense will help you find procedures to follow to get ready for an examination. Too many of us, however, overlook these sensible measures. Indeed, nervousness and fatigue have been found to be the most serious reasons why applicants fail to do their best on civil service tests. Here is a list of reminders:

- Begin your preparation early – Don't wait until the last minute to go scurrying around for books and materials or to find out what the position is all about.
- Prepare continuously – An hour a night for a week is better than an all-night cram session. This has been definitely established. What is more, a night a week for a month will return better dividends than crowding your study into a shorter period of time.
- Locate the place of the exam – You have been sent a notice telling you when and where to report for the examination. If the location is in a different town or otherwise unfamiliar to you, it would be well to inquire the best route and learn something about the building.
- Relax the night before the test – Allow your mind to rest. Do not study at all that night. Plan some mild recreation or diversion; then go to bed early and get a good night's sleep.
- Get up early enough to make a leisurely trip to the place for the test – This way unforeseen events, traffic snarls, unfamiliar buildings, etc. will not upset you.
- Dress comfortably – A written test is not a fashion show. You will be known by number and not by name, so wear something comfortable.
- Leave excess paraphernalia at home – Shopping bags and odd bundles will get in your way. You need bring only the items mentioned in the official notice you received; usually everything you need is provided. Do not bring reference books to the exam. They will only confuse those last minutes and be taken away from you when in the test room.
- Arrive somewhat ahead of time – If because of transportation schedules you must get there very early, bring a newspaper or magazine to take your mind off yourself while waiting.
- Locate the examination room – When you have found the proper room, you will be directed to the seat or part of the room where you will sit. Sometimes you are given a sheet of instructions to read while you are waiting. Do not fill out any forms until you are told to do so; just read them and be prepared.
- Relax and prepare to listen to the instructions
- If you have any physical problem that may keep you from doing your best, be sure to tell the test administrator. If you are sick or in poor health, you really cannot do your best on the exam. You can come back and take the test some other time.

VII. AT THE TEST

The day of the test is here and you have the test booklet in your hand. The temptation to get going is very strong. Caution! There is more to success than knowing the right answers. You must know how to identify your papers and understand variations in the type of short-answer question used in this particular examination. Follow these suggestions for maximum results from your efforts:

1) Cooperate with the monitor

The test administrator has a duty to create a situation in which you can be as much at ease as possible. He will give instructions, tell you when to begin, check to see that you are marking your answer sheet correctly, and so on. He is not there to guard you, although he will see that your competitors do not take unfair advantage. He wants to help you do your best.

2) Listen to all instructions

Don't jump the gun! Wait until you understand all directions. In most civil service tests you get more time than you need to answer the questions. So don't be in a hurry. Read each word of instructions until you clearly understand the meaning. Study the examples, listen to all announcements and follow directions. Ask questions if you do not understand what to do.

3) Identify your papers

Civil service exams are usually identified by number only. You will be assigned a number; you must not put your name on your test papers. Be sure to copy your number correctly. Since more than one exam may be given, copy your exact examination title.

4) Plan your time

Unless you are told that a test is a "speed" or "rate of work" test, speed itself is usually not important. Time enough to answer all the questions will be provided, but this does not mean that you have all day. An overall time limit has been set. Divide the total time (in minutes) by the number of questions to determine the approximate time you have for each question.

5) Do not linger over difficult questions

If you come across a difficult question, mark it with a paper clip (useful to have along) and come back to it when you have been through the booklet. One caution if you do this – be sure to skip a number on your answer sheet as well. Check often to be sure that you have not lost your place and that you are marking in the row numbered the same as the question you are answering.

6) Read the questions

Be sure you know what the question asks! Many capable people are unsuccessful because they failed to *read* the questions correctly.

7) Answer all questions

Unless you have been instructed that a penalty will be deducted for incorrect answers, it is better to guess than to omit a question.

8) Speed tests

It is often better NOT to guess on speed tests. It has been found that on timed tests people are tempted to spend the last few seconds before time is called in marking answers at random – without even reading them – in the hope of picking up a few extra points. To discourage this practice, the instructions may warn you that your score will be "corrected" for guessing. That is, a penalty will be applied. The incorrect answers will be deducted from the correct ones, or some other penalty formula will be used.

9) Review your answers

If you finish before time is called, go back to the questions you guessed or omitted to give them further thought. Review other answers if you have time.

10) Return your test materials

If you are ready to leave before others have finished or time is called, take ALL your materials to the monitor and leave quietly. Never take any test material with you. The monitor can discover whose papers are not complete, and taking a test booklet may be grounds for disqualification.

VIII. EXAMINATION TECHNIQUES

1) Read the general instructions carefully. These are usually printed on the first page of the exam booklet. As a rule, these instructions refer to the timing of the examination; the fact that you should not start work until the signal and must stop work at a signal, etc. If there are any *special* instructions, such as a choice of questions to be answered, make sure that you note this instruction carefully.

2) When you are ready to start work on the examination, that is as soon as the signal has been given, read the instructions to each question booklet, underline any key words or phrases, such as *least, best, outline, describe* and the like. In this way you will tend to answer as requested rather than discover on reviewing your paper that you *listed without describing*, that you selected the *worst* choice rather than the *best* choice, etc.

3) If the examination is of the objective or multiple-choice type – that is, each question will also give a series of possible answers: A, B, C or D, and you are called upon to select the best answer and write the letter next to that answer on your answer paper – it is advisable to start answering each question in turn. There may be anywhere from 50 to 100 such questions in the three or four hours allotted and you can see how much time would be taken if you read through all the questions before beginning to answer any. Furthermore, if you come across a question or group of questions which you know would be difficult to answer, it would undoubtedly affect your handling of all the other questions.

4) If the examination is of the essay type and contains but a few questions, it is a moot point as to whether you should read all the questions before starting to answer any one. Of course, if you are given a choice – say five out of seven and the like – then it is essential to read all the questions so you can eliminate the two that are most difficult. If, however, you are asked to answer all the questions, there may be danger in trying to answer the easiest one first because you may find that you will spend too much time on it. The best technique is to answer the first question, then proceed to the second, etc.

5) Time your answers. Before the exam begins, write down the time it started, then add the time allowed for the examination and write down the time it must be completed, then divide the time available somewhat as follows:

- If 3-1/2 hours are allowed, that would be 210 minutes. If you have 80 objective-type questions, that would be an average of 2-1/2 minutes per question. Allow yourself no more than 2 minutes per question, or a total of 160 minutes, which will permit about 50 minutes to review.
- If for the time allotment of 210 minutes there are 7 essay questions to answer, that would average about 30 minutes a question. Give yourself only 25 minutes per question so that you have about 35 minutes to review.

6) The most important instruction is to *read each question* and make sure you know what is wanted. The second most important instruction is to *time yourself properly* so that you answer every question. The third most important instruction is to *answer every question*. Guess if you have to but include something for each question. Remember that you will receive no credit for a blank and will probably receive some credit if you write something in answer to an essay question. If you guess a letter – say "B" for a multiple-choice question – you may have guessed right. If you leave a blank as an answer to a multiple-choice question, the examiners may respect your feelings but it will not add a point to your score. Some exams may penalize you for wrong answers, so in such cases *only*, you may not want to guess unless you have some basis for your answer.

7) Suggestions
   a. Objective-type questions
      1. Examine the question booklet for proper sequence of pages and questions
      2. Read all instructions carefully
      3. Skip any question which seems too difficult; return to it after all other questions have been answered
      4. Apportion your time properly; do not spend too much time on any single question or group of questions
      5. Note and underline key words – *all, most, fewest, least, best, worst, same, opposite,* etc.
      6. Pay particular attention to negatives
      7. Note unusual option, e.g., unduly long, short, complex, different or similar in content to the body of the question
      8. Observe the use of "hedging" words – *probably, may, most likely,* etc.
      9. Make sure that your answer is put next to the same number as the question
      10. Do not second-guess unless you have good reason to believe the second answer is definitely more correct
      11. Cross out original answer if you decide another answer is more accurate; do not erase until you are ready to hand your paper in
      12. Answer all questions; guess unless instructed otherwise
      13. Leave time for review

   b. Essay questions
      1. Read each question carefully
      2. Determine exactly what is wanted. Underline key words or phrases.
      3. Decide on outline or paragraph answer

4. Include many different points and elements unless asked to develop any one or two points or elements
5. Show impartiality by giving pros and cons unless directed to select one side only
6. Make and write down any assumptions you find necessary to answer the questions
7. Watch your English, grammar, punctuation and choice of words
8. Time your answers; don't crowd material

8) Answering the essay question

Most essay questions can be answered by framing the specific response around several key words or ideas. Here are a few such key words or ideas:

M's: manpower, materials, methods, money, management
P's: purpose, program, policy, plan, procedure, practice, problems, pitfalls, personnel, public relations
   a. Six basic steps in handling problems:
      1. Preliminary plan and background development
      2. Collect information, data and facts
      3. Analyze and interpret information, data and facts
      4. Analyze and develop solutions as well as make recommendations
      5. Prepare report and sell recommendations
      6. Install recommendations and follow up effectiveness

   b. Pitfalls to avoid
      1. *Taking things for granted* – A statement of the situation does not necessarily imply that each of the elements is necessarily true; for example, a complaint may be invalid and biased so that all that can be taken for granted is that a complaint has been registered
      2. *Considering only one side of a situation* – Wherever possible, indicate several alternatives and then point out the reasons you selected the best one
      3. *Failing to indicate follow up* – Whenever your answer indicates action on your part, make certain that you will take proper follow-up action to see how successful your recommendations, procedures or actions turn out to be
      4. *Taking too long in answering any single question* – Remember to time your answers properly

IX. AFTER THE TEST

Scoring procedures differ in detail among civil service jurisdictions although the general principles are the same. Whether the papers are hand-scored or graded by machine we have described, they are nearly always graded by number. That is, the person who marks the paper knows only the number – never the name – of the applicant. Not until all the papers have been graded will they be matched with names. If other tests, such as training and experience or oral interview ratings have been given, scores will be combined. Different parts of the examination usually have different weights. For example, the written test might count 60 percent of the final grade, and a rating of training and experience 40 percent. In many jurisdictions, veterans will have a certain number of points added to their grades.

After the final grade has been determined, the names are placed in grade order and an eligible list is established. There are various methods for resolving ties between those who get the same final grade – probably the most common is to place first the name of the person whose application was received first. Job offers are made from the eligible list in the order the names appear on it. You will be notified of your grade and your rank as soon as all these computations have been made. This will be done as rapidly as possible.

People who are found to meet the requirements in the announcement are called "eligibles." Their names are put on a list of eligible candidates. An eligible's chances of getting a job depend on how high he stands on this list and how fast agencies are filling jobs from the list.

When a job is to be filled from a list of eligibles, the agency asks for the names of people on the list of eligibles for that job. When the civil service commission receives this request, it sends to the agency the names of the three people highest on this list. Or, if the job to be filled has specialized requirements, the office sends the agency the names of the top three persons who meet these requirements from the general list.

The appointing officer makes a choice from among the three people whose names were sent to him. If the selected person accepts the appointment, the names of the others are put back on the list to be considered for future openings.

That is the rule in hiring from all kinds of eligible lists, whether they are for typist, carpenter, chemist, or something else. For every vacancy, the appointing officer has his choice of any one of the top three eligibles on the list. This explains why the person whose name is on top of the list sometimes does not get an appointment when some of the persons lower on the list do. If the appointing officer chooses the second or third eligible, the No. 1 eligible does not get a job at once, but stays on the list until he is appointed or the list is terminated.

X. HOW TO PASS THE INTERVIEW TEST

The examination for which you applied requires an oral interview test. You have already taken the written test and you are now being called for the interview test – the final part of the formal examination.

You may think that it is not possible to prepare for an interview test and that there are no procedures to follow during an interview. Our purpose is to point out some things you can do in advance that will help you and some good rules to follow and pitfalls to avoid while you are being interviewed.

What is an interview supposed to test?

The written examination is designed to test the technical knowledge and competence of the candidate; the oral is designed to evaluate intangible qualities, not readily measured otherwise, and to establish a list showing the relative fitness of each candidate – as measured against his competitors – for the position sought. Scoring is not on the basis of "right" and "wrong," but on a sliding scale of values ranging from "not passable" to "outstanding." As a matter of fact, it is possible to achieve a relatively low score without a single "incorrect" answer because of evident weakness in the qualities being measured.

Occasionally, an examination may consist entirely of an oral test – either an individual or a group oral. In such cases, information is sought concerning the technical knowledges and abilities of the candidate, since there has been no written examination for this purpose. More commonly, however, an oral test is used to supplement a written examination.

Who conducts interviews?

The composition of oral boards varies among different jurisdictions. In nearly all, a representative of the personnel department serves as chairman. One of the members of the board may be a representative of the department in which the candidate would work. In some cases, "outside experts" are used, and, frequently, a businessman or some other representative of the general public is asked to serve. Labor and management or other special groups may be represented. The aim is to secure the services of experts in the appropriate field.

However the board is composed, it is a good idea (and not at all improper or unethical) to ascertain in advance of the interview who the members are and what groups they represent. When you are introduced to them, you will have some idea of their backgrounds and interests, and at least you will not stutter and stammer over their names.

What should be done before the interview?

While knowledge about the board members is useful and takes some of the surprise element out of the interview, there is other preparation which is more substantive. It *is* possible to prepare for an oral interview – in several ways:

1) Keep a copy of your application and review it carefully before the interview

This may be the only document before the oral board, and the starting point of the interview. Know what education and experience you have listed there, and the sequence and dates of all of it. Sometimes the board will ask you to review the highlights of your experience for them; you should not have to hem and haw doing it.

2) Study the class specification and the examination announcement

Usually, the oral board has one or both of these to guide them. The qualities, characteristics or knowledges required by the position sought are stated in these documents. They offer valuable clues as to the nature of the oral interview. For example, if the job involves supervisory responsibilities, the announcement will usually indicate that knowledge of modern supervisory methods and the qualifications of the candidate as a supervisor will be tested. If so, you can expect such questions, frequently in the form of a hypothetical situation which you are expected to solve. NEVER go into an oral without knowledge of the duties and responsibilities of the job you seek.

3) Think through each qualification required

Try to visualize the kind of questions you would ask if you were a board member. How well could you answer them? Try especially to appraise your own knowledge and background in each area, *measured against the job sought*, and identify any areas in which you are weak. Be critical and realistic – do not flatter yourself.

4) Do some general reading in areas in which you feel you may be weak

For example, if the job involves supervision and your past experience has NOT, some general reading in supervisory methods and practices, particularly in the field of human relations, might be useful. Do NOT study agency procedures or detailed manuals. The oral board will be testing your understanding and capacity, not your memory.

5) Get a good night's sleep and watch your general health and mental attitude

You will want a clear head at the interview. Take care of a cold or any other minor ailment, and of course, no hangovers.

What should be done on the day of the interview?

Now comes the day of the interview itself. Give yourself plenty of time to get there. Plan to arrive somewhat ahead of the scheduled time, particularly if your appointment is in the fore part of the day. If a previous candidate fails to appear, the board might be ready for you a bit early. By early afternoon an oral board is almost invariably behind schedule if there are many candidates, and you may have to wait. Take along a book or magazine to read, or your application to review, but leave any extraneous material in the waiting room when you go in for your interview. In any event, relax and compose yourself.

The matter of dress is important. The board is forming impressions about you – from your experience, your manners, your attitude, and your appearance. Give your personal appearance careful attention. Dress your best, but not your flashiest. Choose conservative, appropriate clothing, and be sure it is immaculate. This is a business interview, and your appearance should indicate that you regard it as such. Besides, being well groomed and properly dressed will help boost your confidence.

Sooner or later, someone will call your name and escort you into the interview room. *This is it.* From here on you are on your own. It is too late for any more preparation. But remember, you asked for this opportunity to prove your fitness, and you are here because your request was granted.

What happens when you go in?

The usual sequence of events will be as follows: The clerk (who is often the board stenographer) will introduce you to the chairman of the oral board, who will introduce you to the other members of the board. Acknowledge the introductions before you sit down. Do not be surprised if you find a microphone facing you or a stenotypist sitting by. Oral interviews are usually recorded in the event of an appeal or other review.

Usually the chairman of the board will open the interview by reviewing the highlights of your education and work experience from your application – primarily for the benefit of the other members of the board, as well as to get the material into the record. Do not interrupt or comment unless there is an error or significant misinterpretation; if that is the case, do not hesitate. But do not quibble about insignificant matters. Also, he will usually ask you some question about your education, experience or your present job – partly to get you to start talking and to establish the interviewing "rapport." He may start the actual questioning, or turn it over to one of the other members. Frequently, each member undertakes the questioning on a particular area, one in which he is perhaps most competent, so you can expect each member to participate in the examination. Because time is limited, you may also expect some rather abrupt switches in the direction the questioning takes, so do not be upset by it. Normally, a board member will not pursue a single line of questioning unless he discovers a particular strength or weakness.

After each member has participated, the chairman will usually ask whether any member has any further questions, then will ask you if you have anything you wish to add. Unless you are expecting this question, it may floor you. Worse, it may start you off on an extended, extemporaneous speech. The board is not usually seeking more information. The question is principally to offer you a last opportunity to present further qualifications or to indicate that you have nothing to add. So, if you feel that a significant qualification or characteristic has been overlooked, it is proper to point it out in a sentence or so. Do not compliment the board on the thoroughness of their examination – they have been sketchy, and you know it. If you wish, merely say, "No thank you, I have nothing further to add." This is a point where you can "talk yourself out" of a good impression or fail to present an important bit of information. Remember, *you close the interview yourself.*

The chairman will then say, "That is all, Mr. _____, thank you." Do not be startled; the interview is over, and quicker than you think. Thank him, gather your belongings and take your leave. Save your sigh of relief for the other side of the door.

How to put your best foot forward

Throughout this entire process, you may feel that the board individually and collectively is trying to pierce your defenses, seek out your hidden weaknesses and embarrass and confuse you. Actually, this is not true. They are obliged to make an appraisal of your qualifications for the job you are seeking, and they want to see you in your best light. Remember, they must interview all candidates and a non-cooperative candidate may become a failure in spite of their best efforts to bring out his qualifications. Here are 15 suggestions that will help you:

1) Be natural – Keep your attitude confident, not cocky

If you are not confident that you can do the job, do not expect the board to be. Do not apologize for your weaknesses, try to bring out your strong points. The board is interested in a positive, not negative, presentation. Cockiness will antagonize any board member and make him wonder if you are covering up a weakness by a false show of strength.

2) Get comfortable, but don't lounge or sprawl

Sit erectly but not stiffly. A careless posture may lead the board to conclude that you are careless in other things, or at least that you are not impressed by the importance of the occasion. Either conclusion is natural, even if incorrect. Do not fuss with your clothing, a pencil or an ashtray. Your hands may occasionally be useful to emphasize a point; do not let them become a point of distraction.

3) Do not wisecrack or make small talk

This is a serious situation, and your attitude should show that you consider it as such. Further, the time of the board is limited – they do not want to waste it, and neither should you.

4) Do not exaggerate your experience or abilities

In the first place, from information in the application or other interviews and sources, the board may know more about you than you think. Secondly, you probably will not get away with it. An experienced board is rather adept at spotting such a situation, so do not take the chance.

5) If you know a board member, do not make a point of it, yet do not hide it

Certainly you are not fooling him, and probably not the other members of the board. Do not try to take advantage of your acquaintanceship – it will probably do you little good.

6) Do not dominate the interview

Let the board do that. They will give you the clues – do not assume that you have to do all the talking. Realize that the board has a number of questions to ask you, and do not try to take up all the interview time by showing off your extensive knowledge of the answer to the first one.

7) Be attentive

You only have 20 minutes or so, and you should keep your attention at its sharpest throughout. When a member is addressing a problem or question to you, give him your undivided attention. Address your reply principally to him, but do not exclude the other board members.

8) Do not interrupt

A board member may be stating a problem for you to analyze. He will ask you a question when the time comes. Let him state the problem, and wait for the question.

9) Make sure you understand the question

Do not try to answer until you are sure what the question is. If it is not clear, restate it in your own words or ask the board member to clarify it for you. However, do not haggle about minor elements.

10) Reply promptly but not hastily

A common entry on oral board rating sheets is "candidate responded readily," or "candidate hesitated in replies." Respond as promptly and quickly as you can, but do not jump to a hasty, ill-considered answer.

11) Do not be peremptory in your answers

A brief answer is proper – but do not fire your answer back. That is a losing game from your point of view. The board member can probably ask questions much faster than you can answer them.

12) Do not try to create the answer you think the board member wants

He is interested in what kind of mind you have and how it works – not in playing games. Furthermore, he can usually spot this practice and will actually grade you down on it.

13) Do not switch sides in your reply merely to agree with a board member

Frequently, a member will take a contrary position merely to draw you out and to see if you are willing and able to defend your point of view. Do not start a debate, yet do not surrender a good position. If a position is worth taking, it is worth defending.

14) Do not be afraid to admit an error in judgment if you are shown to be wrong

The board knows that you are forced to reply without any opportunity for careful consideration. Your answer may be demonstrably wrong. If so, admit it and get on with the interview.

15) Do not dwell at length on your present job

The opening question may relate to your present assignment. Answer the question but do not go into an extended discussion. You are being examined for a *new* job, not your present one. As a matter of fact, try to phrase ALL your answers in terms of the job for which you are being examined.

Basis of Rating

Probably you will forget most of these "do's" and "don'ts" when you walk into the oral interview room. Even remembering them all will not ensure you a passing grade. Perhaps you did not have the qualifications in the first place. But remembering them will help you to put your best foot forward, without treading on the toes of the board members.

Rumor and popular opinion to the contrary notwithstanding, an oral board wants you to make the best appearance possible. They know you are under pressure – but they also want to see how you respond to it as a guide to what your reaction would be under the pressures of the job you seek. They will be influenced by the degree of poise you display, the personal traits you show and the manner in which you respond.

ABOUT THIS BOOK

This book contains tests divided into Examination Sections. Go through each test, answering every question in the margin. At the end of each test look at the answer key and check your answers. On the ones you got wrong, look at the right answer choice and learn. Do not fill in the answers first. Do not memorize the questions and answers, but understand the answer and principles involved. On your test, the questions will likely be different from the samples. Questions are changed and new ones added. If you understand these past questions you should have success with any changes that arise. Tests may consist of several types of questions. We have additional books on each subject should more study be advisable or necessary for you. Finally, the more you study, the better prepared you will be. This book is intended to be the last thing you study before you walk into the examination room. Prior study of relevant texts is also recommended. NLC publishes some of these in our Fundamental Series. Knowledge and good sense are important factors in passing your exam. Good luck also helps. So now study this Passbook, absorb the material contained within and take that knowledge into the examination. Then do your best to pass that exam.

EXAMINATION SECTION

EXAMINATION SECTION

TEST 1

DIRECTIONS: Each question or incomplete statement is followed by several suggested answers or completions. Select the one that BEST answers the question or completes the statement. *PRINT THE LETTER OF THE CORRECT ANSWER IN THE SPACE AT THE RIGHT.*

1. The one of the following that is MOST advisable to do before transcribing your dictation notes is to
   A. check the syllabification of long words for typing purposes
   B. edit your notes
   C. number the pages of dictation
   D. sort them by the kind of typing format required

1._____

2. As a secretary, the one of the following which is LEAST important in writing a letter under your own signature is
   A. the accuracy of the information
   B. the appropriateness of the language
   C. the reason for the letter
   D. your supervisor's approval of the final copy

2._____

3. In a typed letter, the reference line is used
   A. for identification purposes on typed pages of more than one page
   B. to indicate under what heading the copy of the letter should be filed
   C. to indicate who dictated the letter and who typed it
   D. to make the subject of the letter prominent by typing it a single space below the salutation

3._____

Questions 4-5:

DIRECTIONS: For questions 4 and 5, choose the letter of the sentence that BEST and MOST clearly expresses its meaning.

4.
   A. It has always been the practice of this office to effectuate recruitment of prospective employees from other departments.
   B. This office has always made a practice of recruiting prospective employees from other departments.
   C. Recruitment of prospective employees from other departments has always been a practice which has been implemented by this office.
   D. Implementation of the policy of recruitment of prospective employees from other departments has always been a practice of this office.

4._____

5.
   A. These employees are assigned to the level of work evidenced by
      their efforts and skills during the training period.
   B. The level of work to which these employees is assigned is
      decided upon on the basis of the efforts and skills evidenced by
      them during the period in which they were trained.
   C. Assignment of these employees is made on the basis of the level
      of work their efforts and skills during the training period has
      evidenced.
   D. These employees are assigned to a level of work their efforts and
      skills during the training period have evidenced.

5._____

6. An office assistant was asked to mail a duplicated report of 100 pages to
a professor in an out-of-town university. The professor sending the report
dictated a short letter that he wanted to mail with the report.
Of the following, the MOST inexpensive proper means of sending these
two items would be to send the report
   A. and the letter first class
   B. by parcel post and the letter separately by air mail
   C. and the letter by parcel post
   D. by parcel post and attach to the package an envelope with first-
      class postage in which is enclosed the letter

6._____

7. Plans are underway to determine the productivity of the typists who work
in a central office. Of the procedures listed, the one generally considered
the MOST accurate for finding out the typists' output is to
   A. keep a record of how much typing is done over specified periods
      of time
   B. ask each typist how fast she types when she is doing a great deal
      of word processing
   C. give each typist a timed test during a specified period
   D. ask the supervisor to estimate the typing speed of each
      subordinate

7._____

8. Assume that an executive regularly receives the four types of mail listed
below.
As a general rule, the executive's secretary should arrange the mail from
top to bottom so that the top items are
   A. advertisements
   B. airmail letters
   C. business letters
   D. unopened personal letters

8._____

9. An office assistant in transcribing reports and letters from dictation should
MOST generally assume that

    A. the transcript should be exactly what was dictated so there is little
need to check any details

    B. the dictated material is merely an idea of what the dictator wanted
to say so changes should be made to improve any part of the
dictation

    C. there may be some slight changes, but essentially the
transcription is to be a faithful copy of what was dictated

    D. the transcript is merely a very rough draft and should be typed
quickly so that the dictator can review it and make changes
preliminary to having the final copy typed

9._____

10. The one of the following which generally is the CHIEF disadvantage of
using office machines in place of human workers in office work is that the
machines are

    A. slower   B. less accurate

    C. more costly   D. less flexible

10._____

11. An office assistant in a New York City college is asked to place a call to a
prospective visiting professor in Los Angeles. It is 1 p.m. in New York
(EST). The time in Los Angeles is

    A. 9 a.m.   B. 10 a.m.   C. 4 p.m.   D. 5 p.m.

11._____

12. An office assistant is instructed to send a copy of a report to a professor
located in a building across campus. The fastest and most efficient way
for this report to reach the professor is by

    A. sending a messenger to hand-deliver it to the professor's office

    B. sending it via fax to the main office of the professor's department

    C. e-mailing it to the professor

    D. dictating the contents of the report to the professor over the phone

12._____

13. An office assistant is in the process of typing the forms for
recommendation for promotion for a member of the faculty who is away
for a week. She notes that two books of which he is the author are listed
without dates.

Of the following, the procedure she should BEST follow at this point
generally is to

    A. postpone doing the job until the professor returns to campus the
following week

    B. type the material omitting the books

    C. check the professor's office for copies of the books and obtain the
correct data

    D. call the professor's wife and ask her when the books were
published

13._____

14. An office has introduced work standards for all of the employees.　　　　14._____
Of the following, it is MOST likely that use of such standards would tend
to
    A. make it more difficult to determine numbers of employees needed
    B. lead to a substantial drop in morale among all of the employees
    C. reduce the possibility of planning to meet emergencies
    D. reduce uncertainty about the costs of doing tasks

15. Of the following clerical errors, the one which probably is LEAST　　　　15._____
important is
    A. adding 543 instead of 548 to a bookkeeping account
    B. putting the wrong code on a data processing card
    C. recording a transaction on the record of Henry Smith instead of on
       the record of Harry Smith
    D. writing John Murpfy instead of John Murphy when addressing an
       envelope

16. Of the following errors, the one which probably is MOST important is　　　16._____
    A. writing "they're" instead of "their" in an office memo
    B. misplacing a decimal point on a sales invoice
    C. forgetting to write the date on a note for a supervisor
    D. sending an e-mail to a misspelled e-mail address

17. The chairman of an academic department tells an office assistant that a　　17._____
meeting of the faculty is to be held four weeks from the current date.
Of the following responsibilities, the office assistant is MOST frequently
held responsible for
    A. planning the agenda of the meeting
    B. presiding over the conduct of the meeting
    C. reserving the meeting room and notifying the members
    D. initiating all formal resolutions

18. Of the following, a centralized filing system is LEAST suitable for filing　　18._____
    A. material which is confidential in nature
    B. routine correspondence
    C. periodic reports of the divisions of the department
    D. material used by several divisions of the department

19. A misplaced record is a lost record.　　　　19._____
Of the following, the MOST valid implication of this statement in regard to
office work is that
    A. all records in an office should be filed in strict alphabetical order
    B. accuracy in filing is essential
    C. only one method of filing should be used throughout the office
    D. files should be locked when not in use

20. When typing names or titles on a roll of folder labels, the one of the following which is MOST important to do is to type the caption

    20._____

    A. as it appears on the papers to be placed in the folder
    B. in capital letters
    C. in exact indexing or filing order
    D. so that it appears near the bottom of the folder tab when the label is attached

21. A professor at a Boston university asks an office assistant to place a call to a fellow professor in San Francisco. The MOST appropriate local time for the assistant to place the call to the professor in California, given the time difference, would be

    21._____

    A. 8:30 a.m.   B. 10:00 a.m.   C. 11:30 a.m.   D. 1:30 p.m.

22. When typing the rough draft of a report, the computer application you would use is

    22._____

    A. Excel   B. Word
    C. PowerPoint   D. Internet Explorer

23. Which of the following is the BEST and most appropriate way to proofread and edit a report before submitting it to a supervisor for review?

    23._____

    A. Scan the report with the program's spell check feature
    B. Proof the report yourself, then ask another office assistant to read the report over as well until it is finished
    C. Give the report to another office assistant who is more skilled at proofreading
    D. Use the spell checker, then scan the report yourself as many times as needed in order to pick up any additional errors

24. The one of the following situations in which it would be MOST justifiable for an office to use standard or form paragraphs in its business letters is when

    24._____

    A. a large number of similar letters is to be sent
    B. the letters are to be uniform in length and appearance
    C. it is desired to reduce typing errors in correspondence
    D. the office is to carry on a lengthy correspondence with an individual

25. Of the following, the MOST important factor in determining whether or not an office filing system is effective is that the

    25._____

    A. information in the files is legible
    B. records in the files are used frequently
    C. information in the files is accurate
    D. records in the files can be located readily

KEY (CORRECT ANSWERS)

1. B	11. B	21. D
2. D	12. C	22. B
3. C	13. C	23. D
4. B	14. D	24. A
5. A	15. D	25. D
6. D	16. B	
7. A	17. C	
8. D	18. A	
9. C	19. B	
10. D	20. C	

TEST 2

DIRECTIONS: Each question or incomplete statement is followed by several suggested answers or completions. Select the one that BEST answers the question or completes the statement. *PRINT THE LETTER OF THE CORRECT ANSWER IN THE SPACE AT THE RIGHT.*

1. For the office assistant whose duties include frequent recording and transcription of minutes of formal meetings, the one of the following reference works generally considered to be MOST useful is
   A. *Robert's Rules of Order*
   B. *Bartlett's Familiar Quotations*
   C. *World Almanac and Book of Facts*
   D. *Conway's Reference*

   1._____

2. Of the following statements about the numeric system of filing, the one which is CORRECT is that it
   A. is the least accurate of all methods of filing
   B. eliminates the need for cross-referencing
   C. allows for very limited expansion
   D. requires a separate index

   2._____

3. When more than one name or subject is involved in a piece of correspondence to be filed, the office assistant should GENERALLY
   A. prepare a cross-reference sheet
   B. establish a geographical filing system
   C. prepare out-guides
   D. establish a separate index card file for noting such correspondence

   3._____

4. A tickler file is MOST generally used for
   A. identification of material contained in a numeric file
   B. maintenance of a current listing of telephone numbers
   C. follow-up of matters requiring future attention
   D. control of records borrowed or otherwise removed from the files

   4._____

5. In filing, the name Ms. *Ann Catalana-Moss* should GENERALLY be indexed as
   A. Moss, Catalana, Ann (Ms.)
   B. Catalana-Moss, Ann (Ms.)
   C. Ann Catalana-Moss (Ms.)
   D. Moss-Catalana, Ann (Ms.)

   5._____

6. An office assistant has a set of four cards, each of which contains one of   6._____
   the following names.
   In alphabetic filing, the FIRST of the cards to be filed is
      A. Ms. Alma John
      B. Mrs. John (Patricia) Edwards
      C. John-Edward School Supplies, Inc.
      D. John H. Edwards

7. Generally, of the following, the name to be filed FIRST in an alphabetical   7._____
   filing system is
      A. Diane Maestro   B. Diana McElroy
      C. James Mackell   D. James McKell

8. After checking several times, you are unable to locate a student record in   8._____
   its proper file drawer. The file drawer in question is used constantly by
   many members of the staff.
   In this situation, the NEXT step you should take in locating the missing
   record is to
      A. ask another worker to look through the file drawer
      B. determine if there is another copy of the record filed in a different
         place
      C. find out if the record has been removed by another staff member
      D. wait a day or two and see if the record turns up

9. It is MOST important that an enclosure which is to be mailed with a letter   9._____
   should be put in an envelope so that
      A. any printing on the enclosure will not be visible through the
         address side of the envelope
      B. it is obvious that there is an enclosure inside the envelope
      C. the enclosure takes up less space than the letter
      D. the person who opens the envelope will pull out both the letter and
         the enclosure

10. Suppose that one of the student aides with whom you work suggests a   10._____
    change in the filing procedure. He is sure the change will result in
    increased rates of filing among the other employees.
    The one of the following which you should do FIRST is to
      A. ask him to demonstrate his method in order to determine if he files
         more quickly than the other employees
      B. ask your supervisor if you may make a change in the filing
         procedure
      C. ignore the aide's suggestion since he is not a filing expert
      D. tell him to show his method to the other employees and to
         encourage them to use it

11. It is generally advisable to leave at least six inches of working space in a
file drawer. This procedure is MOST useful in
   A. decreasing the number of filing errors
   B. facilitating the sorting of documents and folders
   C. maintaining a regular program of removing inactive records
   D. preventing folders and papers from being torn

11._____

12. Assume that a dictator is briefly interrupted because of a telephone call or
other similar matter (no more than three minutes).
Of the following tasks, the person taking the dictation should NORMALLY
use the time to
   A. re-read notes already recorded
   B. tidy the dictator's desk
   C. check the accuracy of the dictator's desk files
   D. return to her own desk to type the dictated material

12._____

13. When typing a preliminary draft of a report, the one of the following which
you should generally NOT do is
   A. erase typing errors and deletions rather than cross them out
   B. leave plenty of room at the top, bottom and sides of each page
   C. make only the number of copies that you are asked to make
   D. type double or triple space

13._____

14. The BEST way for a receptionist to deal with a situation in which she
must leave her desk for a long time is to
   A. ask someone to take her place while she is away
   B. leave a note or sign on her desk which indicates the time she will
       return
   C. take a chance that no one will arrive while she is gone and leave
       her desk unattended
   D. tell a coworker to ask any visitors that arrive to wait until she
       returns

14._____

15. Suppose that two individuals come up to your desk at the same time.
One of them asks you for the location of the nearest public phone. After
you answer the question, you turn to the second person who asks you the
same question.
The one of the following actions that would be BEST for you to take in this
situation is to
   A. ignore the second person since he obviously overheard your first
       answer
   B. point out that you just answered the same question and quickly
       repeat the information
   C. politely repeat the information to the second individual
   D. tell the second person to follow the first to the public telephone

15._____

16. Which of the following names should be filed FIRST in an alphabetical filing system?

    A. Anthony Aarvedsen   B. William Aaron
    C. Denise Aron   D. A.J. Arrington

16._____

17. New material added to a file folder should USUALLY be inserted

    A. in the order of importance (the most important in front)
    B. in the order of importance (the most important in back)
    C. chronologically (most recent in front)
    D. chronologically (most recent in back)

17._____

18. An individual is looking for a name in the White Pages of a telephone directory.
    Which of the following BEST describes the system of filing found there?

    A. alphabetic   B. sequential
    C. locator   D. index

18._____

19. The MAIN purpose of a tickler file is to

    A. help prevent overlooking matters that require future attention
    B. check on adequacy of past performance
    C. pinpoint responsibility for recurring daily tasks
    D. reduce the volume of material kept in general files

19._____

20. Which of the following BEST describes the process of *reconciling* a bank statement?

    A. Analyzing the nature of the expenditures made by the office during the preceding month
    B. Comparing the statement of the bank with the banking records maintained in the office
    C. Determining the liquidity position by reading the bank statement carefully
    D. Checking the service charges noted on the bank statement

20._____

21. From the viewpoint of preserving agency or institutional funds, the LEAST acceptable method for making a payment is a check made out to

    A. cash   B. a company
    C. an individual   D. a partnership

21._____

22. Listed below are four of the steps in the process of preparing correspondence for filing.
    If they were to be put in logical sequence, the SECOND step would be

    A. preparing cross-reference sheets or cards
    B. coding the correspondence using a classification system
    C. sorting the correspondence in the order to be filed
    D. checking for follow-up action required and preparing a follow-up slip

22._____

23. The process of *justifying* typed copy involves laying out the copy so that 23._____
    A. each paragraph appears to be approximately the same size
    B. no long words are broken up at the end of a line
    C. the right and left hand margins are even
    D. there is enough room to enter proofreading marks at the end of each line

24. The MOST important reason for a person in charge of a petty cash fund to obtain receipts for payments is that this practice would tend to 24._____
    A. decrease robberies by delivery personnel
    B. eliminate the need to keep a record of petty cash expenditures
    C. prove that the fund has been used properly
    D. provide a record of the need for cash in the daily operations of the office

25. You should GENERALLY replenish a petty cash fund 25._____
    A. at regularly established intervals
    B. each time you withdraw a sum
    C. when the amount of cash gets below a certain specified amount
    D. when the fund is completely empty

KEY (CORRECT ANSWERS)

1. A	11. D	21. A
2. D	12. A	22. A
3. A	13. A	23. C
4. C	14. A	24. C
5. B	15. C	25. C
6. D	16. B	
7. C	17. C	
8. C	18. A	
9. D	19. A	
10. A	20. B	

EXAMINATION SECTION
TEST 1

DIRECTIONS: Each question or incomplete statement is followed by several suggested answers or completions. Select the one that BEST answers the question or completes the statement. *PRINT THE LETTER OF THE CORRECT ANSWER IN THE SPACE AT THE RIGHT.*

1. Assume that a few co-workers meet near your desk and talk about personal matters during working hours. Lately, this practice has interfered with your work.
   In order to stop this practice, the BEST action for you to take FIRST is to

    1._____

   A. ask your supervisor to put a stop to the co-workers' meeting near your desk
   B. discontinue any friendship with this group
   C. ask your co-workers not to meet near your desk
   D. request that your desk be moved to another location

2. In order to maintain office coverage during working hours, your supervisor has scheduled your lunch hour from 1 P.M. to 2 P.M. and your co-worker's lunch hour from 12 P.M. to 1 P.M. Lately, your co-worker has been returning late from lunch each day. As a result, you don't get a full hour since you must return to the office by 2 P.M.
   Of the following, the BEST action for you to take FIRST is to

    2._____

   A. explain to your co-worker in a courteous manner that his lateness is interfering with your right to a full hour for lunch
   B. tell your co-worker that his lateness must stop or you will report him to your supervisor
   C. report your co-worker's lateness to your supervisor
   D. leave at 1 P.M. for lunch, whether your co-worker has returned or not

3. Assume that, as an office worker, one of your jobs is to open mail sent to your unit, read the mail for content, and send the mail to the appropriate person to handle. You accidentally open and begin to read a letter marked *personal* addressed to a co-worker.
   Of the following, the BEST action for you to take is to

    3._____

   A. report to your supervisor that your co-worker is receiving personal mail at the office
   B. destroy the letter so that your co-worker does not know you saw it
   C. reseal the letter and place it on the co-worker's desk without saying anything
   D. bring the letter to your co-worker and explain that you opened it by accident

4. Suppose that in evaluating your work, your supervisor gives you an overall good rating, but states that you sometimes turn in work with careless errors.
   The BEST action for you to take would be to

    4._____

   A. ask a co-worker who is good at details to proofread your work
   B. take time to do a careful job, paying more attention to detail
   C. continue working as usual since occasional errors are to be expected
   D. ask your supervisor if she would mind correcting your errors

5. Assume that you are taking a telephone message for a co-worker who is not in the office at the time.
   Of the following, the LEAST important item to write on the message is the

    5._____

   A. length of the call
   B. name of the caller
   C. time of the call
   D. telephone number of the caller

Questions 6-13.

DIRECTIONS: Questions 6 through 13 each consist of a sentence which may or may not be an example of good English. The underlined parts of each sentence may be correct or incorrect. Examine each sentence, considering grammar, punctuation, spelling, and capitalization. If the English usage in the underlined parts of the sentence given is better than any of the changes in the underlined words suggested in Options B, C, or D, choose Option A. If the changes in the underlined words suggested in Options B, C, or D would make the sentence correct, choose the correct option. Do not choose an option that will change the meaning of the sentence.

6.   This Fall, the office will be closed on Columbus Day, October 9th.   6._____

    A.   Correct as is
    B.   fall...Columbus Day, October
    C.   Fall...columbus day, October
    D.   fall...Columbus Day, october

7.   This manual discribes the duties performed by an Office Aide.   7._____

    A.   Correct as is
    B.   describe the duties performed
    C.   discribe the duties performed
    D.   describes the duties performed

8.   There weren't no paper in the supply closet.   8._____

    A.   Correct as is   B.   weren't any
    C.   wasn't any   D.   wasn't no

9.   The new employees left there office to attend a meeting.   9._____

    A.   Correct as is   B.   they're
    C.   their   D.   thier

10.   The office worker started working at 8:30 a.m.   10._____

    A.   Correct as is   B.   8:30 a.m.
    C.   8;30 a,m.   D.   8:30 am

11.   The alphabet, or A to Z sequence are the basis of most filing systems.   11._____

    A.   Correct as is
    B.   alphabet, or A to Z sequence, is
    C.   alphabet, or A to Z sequence are
    D.   alphabet, or A too Z sequence, is

12.   Those file cabinets are five feet tall.   12._____

    A.   Correct as is   B.   Them...feet
    C.   Those...foot   D.   Them...foot

13. The Office Aide checked the <u>register and finding</u> the date of the meeting.   13._____

    A. Correct as is   B. regaster and finding
    C. register and found   D. regaster and found

Questions 14-21.

DIRECTIONS: Each of Questions 14 through 21 has two lists of numbers. Each list contains three sets of numbers. Check each of the three sets in the list on the right to see if they are the same as the corresponding set in the list on the left. Mark your answers:

    A. If none of the sets in the right list are the same as those in the left list
    B. if only one of the sets in the right list are the same as those in the left list
    C. if only two of the sets in the right list are the same as those in the left list
    D. if all three sets in the right list are the same as those in the left list

14. 7354183476   7354983476   14._____
     4474747744   4474747774
     57914302311   57914302311

15. 7143592185   7143892185   15._____
     8344517699   8344518699
     9178531263   9178531263

16. 2572114731   257214731   16._____
     8806835476   8806835476
     8255831246   8255831246

17. 331476853821   331476858621   17._____
     6976658532996   6976655832996
     3766042113715   3766042113745

18. 8806663315   8806663315   18._____
     74477138449   74477138449
     211756663666   211756663666

19. 990006966996   99000696996   19._____
     53022219743   53022219843
     4171171117717   4171171177717

20. 24400222433004   24400222433004   20._____
     5300030055000355   5300030055500355
     20000075532002022   20000075532002022

21. 6111666406600001116   61116664066001116   21._____
     7111300117001100733   7111300117001100733
     26666446664476518   26666446664476518

Questions 22-25.

DIRECTIONS: Each of Questions 22 through 25 has two lists of names and addresses. Each list contains three sets of names and addresses. Check each of the three sets in the list on the right to see if they are the same as the corresponding set in the list on the left. Mark your answers:
- A.   if none of the sets in the right list are the same as those in the left list
- B.   if only one of the sets in the right list is the same as those in the left list
- C.   if only two of the sets in the right list are the same as those in the left list
- D.   if all three sets in the right list are the same as those in the left list

22.   Mary T. Berlinger
2351 Hampton St.
Monsey, N.Y. 20117

      Eduardo Benes
473 Kingston Avenue
Central Islip, N.Y. 11734

      Alan Carrington Fuchs
17 Gnarled Hollow Road
Los Angeles, CA 91635

      Mary T. Berlinger
2351 Hampton St.
Monsey, N.Y. 20117

      Eduardo Benes
473 Kingston Avenue
Central Islip, N.Y. 11734

      Alan Carrington Fuchs
17 Gnarled Hollow Road
Los Angeles, CA 91685

22._____

23.   David John Jacobson
178 35 St. Apt. 4C
New York, N.Y. 00927

      Ann-Marie Calonella
7243 South Ridge Blvd.
Bakersfield, CA 96714

      Pauline M. Thompson
872 Linden Ave.
Houston, Texas 70321

      David John Jacobson
178 53 St. Apt. 4C
New York, N.Y. 00927

      Ann-Marie Calonella
7243 South Ridge Blvd.
Bakersfield, CA 96714

      Pauline M. Thomson
872 Linden Ave.
Houston, Texas 70321

23._____

24.   Chester LeRoy Masterton
152 Lacy Rd.
Kankakee, Ill. 54532

      William Maloney
S. LaCrosse Pla.
Wausau, Wisconsin 52146

      Cynthia V. Barnes
16 Pines Rd.
Greenpoint, Miss. 20376

      Chester LeRoy Masterson
152 Lacy Rd.
Kankakee, Ill. 54532

      William Maloney
S. LaCross Pla.
Wausau, Wisconsin 52146

      Cynthia V. Barnes
16 Pines Rd.
Greenpoint, Miss. 20376

24._____

25.　Marcel Jean Frontenac
　　　6 Burton On The Water
　　　Calender, Me. 01471

　　　J. Scott Marsden
　　　174 S. Tipton St.
　　　Cleveland, Ohio

　　　Lawrence T. Haney
　　　171 McDonough St.
　　　Decatur, Ga. 31304

Marcel Jean Frontenac
6 Burton On The Water
Calender, Me. 01471

J. Scott Marsden
174 Tipton St.
Cleveland, Ohio

Lawrence T. Haney
171 McDonough St.
Decatur, Ga. 31304

25.____

KEY (CORRECT ANSWERS)

1. C	11. B
2. A	12. A
3. D	13. C
4. B	14. B
5. A	15. B
6. A	16. C
7. D	17. A
8. C	18. D
9. C	19. A
10. B	20. C

21. C
22. C
23. B
24. B
25. C

TEST 2

DIRECTIONS: Each question or incomplete statement is followed by several suggested answers or completions. Select the one that BEST answers the question or completes the statement. *PRINT THE LETTER OF THE CORRECT ANSWER IN THE SPACE AT THE RIGHT.*

Questions 1-6.

DIRECTIONS: Questions 1 through 6 are to be answered SOLELY on the basis of the information contained in the following passage.

Duplicating is the process of making a number of identical copies of letters, documents, etc. from an original. Some duplicating processes make copies directly from the original document. Other duplicating processes require the preparation of a special master, and copies are then made from the master. Four of the most common duplicating processes are stencil, fluid, offset, and xerox.

In the stencil process, the typewriter is used to cut the words into a master called a stencil. Drawings, charts, or graphs can be cut into the stencil using a stylus. As many as 3,500 good-quality copies can be reproduced from one stencil. Various grades of finished paper from inexpensive mimeograph to expensive bond can be used.

The fluid process is a good method of copying from 50 to 125 good-quality copies from a master, which is prepared with a special dye. The master is placed on the duplicator, and special paper with a hard finish is moistened and then passed through the duplicator. Some of the dye on the master is dissolved, creating an impression on the paper. The impression becomes lighter as more copies are made; and once the dye on the master is used up, a new master must be made.

The offset process is the most adaptable office duplicating process because this process can be used for making a few copies or many copies. Masters can be made on paper or plastic for a few hundred copies, or on metal plates for as many as 75,000 copies. By using a special technique called photo-offset, charts, photographs, illustrations, or graphs can be reproduced on the master plate. The offset process is capable of producing large quantities of fine, top-quality copies on all types of finished paper.

The xerox process reproduces an exact duplicate from an original. It is the fastest duplicating method because the original material is placed directly on the duplicator, eliminating the need to make a special master. Any kind of paper can be used. The xerox process is the most expensive duplicating process; however, it is the best method of reproducing small quantities of good-quality copies of reports, letters, official documents, memos, or contracts.

1. Of the following, the MOST efficient method of reproducing 5,000 copies of a graph is   1.____

    A. stencil   B. fluid   C. offset   D. xerox

2. The offset process is the MOST adaptable office duplicating process because   2.____

    A. it is the quickest duplicating method
    B. it is the least expensive duplicating method
    C. it can produce a small number or large number of copies
    D. a softer master can be used over and over again

3. Which one of the following duplicating processes uses moistened paper?   3._____

   A. Stencil   B. Fluid   C. Offset   D. Xerox

4. The fluid process would be the BEST process to use for reproducing   4._____

   A. five copies of a school transcript
   B. fifty copies of a memo
   C. five hundred copies of a form letter
   D. five thousand copies of a chart

5. Which one of the following duplicating processes does NOT require a special master?   5._____

   A. Fluid   B. Xerox   C. Offset   D. Stencil

6. Xerox is NOT used for all duplicating jobs because   6._____

   A. it produces poor-quality copies
   B. the process is too expensive
   C. preparing the master is too time-consuming
   D. it cannot produce written reports

7. Assume a city agency has 775 office workers.   7._____
   If 2 out of 25 office workers were absent on a particular day, how many office workers reported to work on that day?

   A. 713   B. 744   C. 750   D. 773

Questions 8-11.

DIRECTIONS: In Questions 8 through 11, select the choice that is CLOSEST in meaning to the underlined word.

SAMPLE: This division reviews the fiscal reports of the agency.
                In this sentence, the word fiscal means MOST NEARLY
                A. financial   B. critical   C. basic   D. personnel

         The correct answer is A, financial, because financial is closest to fiscal.

8. A central file eliminates the need to retain duplicate material.   8._____
   The word retain means MOST NEARLY

   A. keep   B. change   C. locate   D. process

9. Filing is a routine office task.   9._____
   Routine means MOST NEARLY

   A. proper   B. regular   C. simple   D. difficult

10. Sometimes a word, phrase, or sentence must be deleted to correct an error.   10._____
   Deleted means MOST NEARLY

   A. removed   B. added   C. expanded   D. improved

11. Your supervisor will <u>evaluate</u> your work.
<u>Evaluate</u> means MOST NEARLY

11.____

    A. judge   B. list   C. assign   D. explain

Questions 12-19.

DIRECTIONS: The code table below shows 10 letters with matching numbers. For each Question 12 through 19, there are three sets of letters. Each set of letters is followed by a set of numbers which may or may not match their correct letter according to the code table. For each question, check all three sets of letters and numbers and mark your answer:
     A. if no pairs are correctly matched
     B. if only one pair is correctly matched
     C. if only two pairs are correctly matched
     D. if all three pairs are correctly matched

<u>CODE TABLE</u>

T	M	V	D	S	P	R	G	B	H
1	2	3	4	5	6	7	8	9	0

<u>Sample Question:</u>   TMVDSP - 123456
                     RGBHTM - 789011
                     DSPRGB - 256789

In the sample question above, the first set of numbers correctly matches its set of letters. But the second and third pairs contain mistakes. In the second pair, M is incorrectly matched with number 1. According to the code table, letter M should be correctly matched with number 2. In the third pair, the letter D is incorrectly matched with number 2. According to the code table, letter D should be correctly matched with number 4. Since only one of the pairs is correctly matched, the answer to this sample question is B.

12.   RSBMRM -   759262
      GDSRVH -   845730
      VDBRTM -   349713

12.____

13.   TGVSDR -   183247
      SMHRDP -   520647
      TRMHSR -   172057

13.____

14.   DSPRGM -   456782
      MVDBHT -   234902
      HPMDBT -   062491

14.____

15.   BVPTRD -   936184
      GDPHMB -   807029
      GMRHMV -   827032

15.____

16.   MGVRSH -   283750
      TRDMBS -   174295
      SPRMGV -   567283

16.____

17.   SGBSDM - 489542   17.____
       MGHPTM - 290612
       MPBMHT - 269301

18.   TDPBHM - 146902   18.____
       VPBMRS - 369275
       GDMBHM - 842902

19.   MVPTBV - 236194   19.____
       PDRTMB - 647128
       BGTMSM - 981232

Questions 20-25.

DIRECTIONS: In each of Questions 20 through 25, the names of four people are given. For each question, choose as your answer the one of the four names given which should be filed FIRST according to the usual system of alphabetical filing of names, as described in the following paragraph.

In filing names, you must start with the last name. Names are filed in order of the first letter of the last name, then the second letter, etc. Therefore, BAILY would be filed before BROWN, which would be filed before COLT. A name with fewer letters of the same type comes first; i.e., Smith before Smithe. If the last names are the same, the names are filed alphabetically by the first name. If the first name is an initial, a name with an initial would come before a first name that starts with the same letter as the initial. Therefore, I. BROWN would come before IRA BROWN. Finally, if both last name and first name are the same, the name would be filed alphabetically by the middle name, one again an initial coming before a middle name which starts with the same letter as the initial. If there is no middle name at all, the name would come before those with middle initials or names.

Sample Question: A. Lester Daniels
                        B. William Dancer
                        C. Nathan Danzig
                        D. Dan Lester

The last names beginning with D are filed before the last name beginning with L. Since DANIELS, DANCER, and DANZIG all begin with the same three letters, you must look at the fourth letter of the last name to determine which name should be filed first. C comes before I or Z in the alphabet, so DANCER is filed before DANIELS or DANZIG. Therefore, the answer to the above sample question is B.

20.   A. Scott Biala   B. Mary Byala   20.____
      C. Martin Baylor   D. Francis Bauer

21.   A. Howard J. Black   B. Howard Black   21.____
      C. J. Howard Black   D. John H. Black

22.   A. Theodora Garth Kingston   B. Theadore Barth Kingston 22.____
      C. Thomas Kingston   D. Thomas T. Kingston

23.   A. Paulette Mary Huerta   B. Paul M. Huerta   23.____
      C. Paulette L. Huerta   D. Peter A. Huerta

24. A. Martha Hunt Morgan   B. Martin Hunt Morgan   24.____
     C. Mary H. Morgan   D. Martine H. Morgan

25. A. James T. Meerschaum   B. James M. Mershum   25.____
     C. James F. Mearshaum   D. James N. Meshum

KEY (CORRECT ANSWERS)

1. C		11. A	
2. C		12. B	
3. B		13. B	
4. B		14. C	
5. B		15. A	
6. B		16. D	
7. A		17. A	
8. A		18. D	
9. B		19. A	
10. A		20. D	

21. B
22. B
23. B
24. A
25. C

TEST 3

DIRECTIONS: Each question or incomplete statement is followed by several suggested answers or completions. Select the one that BEST answers the question or completes the statement. *PRINT THE LETTER OF THE CORRECT ANSWER IN THE SPACE AT THE RIGHT.*

1. Which one of the following statements about proper telephone usage is NOT always correct?
   When answering the telephone, you should

   A. know whom you are speaking to
   B. give the caller your undivided attention
   C. identify yourself to the caller
   D. obtain the information the caller wishes before you do your other work

   1.____

2. Assume that, as a member of a worker's safety committee in your agency, you are responsible for encouraging other employees to follow correct safety practices. While you are working on your regular assignment, you observe an employee violating a safety rule.
   Of the following, the BEST action for you to take FIRST is to

   A. speak to the employee about safety practices and order him to stop violating the safety rule
   B. speak to the employee about safety practices and point out the safety rule he is violating
   C. bring the matter up in the next committee meeting
   D. report this violation of the safety rule to the employee's supervisor

   2.____

3. Assume that you have been temporarily assigned by your supervisor to do a job which you do not want to do. The BEST action for you to take is to

   A. discuss the job with your supervisor, explaining why you do not want to do it
   B. discuss the job with your supervisor and tell her that you will not do it
   C. ask a co-worker to take your place on this job
   D. do some other job that you like; your supervisor may give the job you do not like to someone else

   3.____

4. Assume that you keep the confidential personnel files of employees in your unit. A friend asks you to obtain some information from the file of one of your co-workers.
   The BEST action to take is to _____ to your friend.

   A. ask the co-worker if you can give the information
   B. ask your supervisor if you can give the information
   C. give the information
   D. refuse to give the information

   4.____

Questions 5-8.

DIRECTIONS: Questions 5 through 8 are to be answered SOLELY on the basis of the information contained in the following passage.

23

City government is committed to providing a safe and healthy work environment for all city employees. An effective agency safety program reduces accidents by educating employees about the types of careless acts which can cause accidents. Even in an office, accidents can happen. If each employee is aware of possible safety hazards, the number of accidents on the job can be reduced.

Careless use of office equipment can cause accidents and injuries. For example, file cabinet drawers which are filled with papers can be so heavy that the entire cabinet could tip over from the weight of one open drawer.

The bottom drawers of desks and file cabinets should never be left open since employees could easily trip over open drawers and injure themselves.

When reaching for objects on a high shelf, an employee should use a strong, sturdy object such as a step stool to stand on. Makeshift platforms made out of books, papers, or boxes can easily collapse. Even chairs can slide out from under foot, causing serious injury.

Even at an employee's desk, safety hazards can occur. Frayed or cut wires should be repaired or replaced immediately. Computers which are not firmly anchored to the desk or table could fall, causing injury.

Smoking is one of the major causes of fires in the office. A lighted match or improperly extinguished cigarette thrown into a wastebasket filled with paper could cause a major fire with possible loss of life. Where smoking is permitted, ashtrays should be used. Smoking is particularly dangerous in offices where flammable chemicals are used.

5. The goal of an effective safety program is to　　5._____

    A. reduce office accidents
    B. stop employees from smoking on the job
    C. encourage employees to continue their education
    D. eliminate high shelves in offices

6. Desks and file cabinets can become safety hazards when　　6._____

    A. their drawers are left open
    B. they are used as wastebaskets
    C. they are makeshift
    D. they are not anchored securely to the floor

7. Smoking is especially hazardous when it occurs　　7._____

    A. near exposed wires
    B. in a crowded office
    C. in an area where flammable chemicals are used
    D. where books and papers are stored

8. Accidents are likely to occur when　　8._____

    A. employees' desks are cluttered with books and papers
    B. employees are not aware of safety hazards
    C. employees close desk drawers
    D. step stools are used to reach high objects

9. Assume that part of your job as a worker in the accounting division of a city agency is to answer the telephone. When you first answer the telephone, it is LEAST important to tell the caller

    A. your title   B. your name
    C. the name of your unit   D. the name of your agency

9.____

10. Assume that you are assigned to work as a receptionist, and your duties are to answer phones, greet visitors, and do other general office work. You are busy with a routine job when several visitors approach your desk.
The BEST action to take is to

    A. ask the visitors to have a seat and assist them after your work is completed
    B. tell the visitors that you are busy and they should return at a more convenient time
    C. stop working long enough to assist the visitors
    D. continue working and wait for the visitors to ask you for assistance

10.____

11. Assume that your supervisor has chosen you to take a special course during working hours to learn a new payroll procedure. Although you know that you were chosen because of your good work record, a co-worker, who feels that he should have been chosen, has been telling everyone in your unit that the choice was unfair.
Of the following, the BEST way to handle this situation FIRST is to

    A. suggest to the co-worker that everything in life is unfair
    B. contact your union representative in case your co-worker presents a formal grievance
    C. tell your supervisor about your co-worker's complaints and let her handle the situation
    D. tell the co-worker that you were chosen because of your superior work record

11.____

12. Assume that while you are working on an assignment which must be completed quickly, a supervisor from another unit asks you to obtain information for her.
Of the following, the BEST way to respond to her request is to

    A. tell her to return in an hour since you are busy
    B. give her the names of some people in her own unit who could help her
    C. tell her you are busy and refer her to a co-worker
    D. tell her that you are busy and ask her if she could wait until you finish your assignment

12.____

13. A co-worker in your unit is often off from work because of illness. Your supervisor assigns the co-worker's work to you when she is not there. Lately, doing her work has interfered with your own job.
The BEST action for you to take FIRST is to

    A. discuss the problem with your supervisor
    B. complete your own work before starting your co-worker's work
    C. ask other workers in your unit to assist you
    D. work late in order to get the jobs done

13.____

14. During the month of June, 40,587 people attended a city-owned swimming pool. In July, 13,014 more people attended the swimming pool than the number that had attended in June. In August, 39,655 people attended the swimming pool.
The TOTAL number of people who attended the swimming pool during the months of June, July, and August was

    A. 80,242   B. 93,256   C. 133,843   D. 210,382

14.____

Questions 15-22.

DIRECTIONS: Questions 15 through 22 test how well you understand what you read. It will be necessary for you to read carefully because your answers to these questions must be based ONLY on the information in the following paragraphs.

The telephone directory is made up of two books. The first book consists of the introductory section and the alphabetical listing of names section. The second book is the classified directory (also known as the yellow pages). Many people who are familiar with one book do not realize how useful the other can be. The efficient office worker should become familiar with both books in order to make the best use of this important source of information.

The introductory section gives general instructions for finding numbers in the alphabetical listing and classified directory. This section also explains how to use the telephone company's many services, including the operator and information services, gives examples of charges for local and long-distance calls, and lists area codes for the entire country. In addition, this section provides a useful postal zip code map.

The alphabetical listing of names section lists the names, addresses, and telephone numbers of subscribers in an area. Guide names, or *telltales*, are on the top corner of each page. These guide names indicate the first and last name to be found on that page. *Telltales* help locate any particular name quickly. A cross-reference spelling is also given to help locate names which are spelled several different ways. City, state, and federal government agencies are listed under the major government heading. For example, an agency of the federal government would be listed under *United States Government.*

The classified directory, or yellow pages, is a separate book. In this section are advertising services, public transportation line maps, shopping guides, and listings of businesses arranged by the type of product or services they offer. This book is most useful when looking for the name or phone number of a business when all that is known is the type of product offered and the address, or when trying to locate a particular type of business in an area. Businesses listed in the classified directory can usually be found in the alphabetical listing of names section. When the name of the business is known, you will find the address or phone number more quickly in the alphabetical listing of names section.

15. The introductory section provides

    A. shopping guides   B. government listings
    C. business listings   D. information services

15.____

16. Advertising services would be found in the

    A. introductory section   B. alphabetical listing of names section
    C. classified directory   D. information services

16.____

17. According to the information in the above passage for locating government agencies, the   17.____
    Information Office of the Department of Consumer Affairs of New York City government
    would be alphabetically listed FIRST under

    A. *I* for Information Offices
    B. *D* for Department of Consumer Affairs
    C. *N* for New York City
    D. *G* for government

18. When the name of a business is known, the QUICKEST way to find the phone number is   18.____
    to look in the

    A. classified directory
    B. introductory section
    C. alphabetical listing of names section
    D. advertising service section

19. The QUICKEST way to find the phone number of a business when the type of service a   19.____
    business offers and its address is known is to look in the

    A. classified directory
    B. alphabetical listing of names section
    C. introductory section
    D. information service

20. What is a *telltale?*   20.____

    A. An alphabetical listing
    B. A guide name
    C. A map
    D. A cross-reference listing

21. The BEST way to find a postal zip code is to look in the   21.____

    A. classified directory
    B. introductory section
    C. alphabetical listing of names section
    D. government heading

22. To help find names which have several different spellings, the telephone directory pro-   22.____
    vides

    A. cross-reference spelling   B. *telltales*
    C. spelling guides   D. advertising services

23. Assume that your agency has been given $2025 to purchase file cabinets.   23.____
    If each file cabinet costs $135, how many file cabinets can your agency purchase?

    A. 8   B. 10   C. 15   D. 16

24. Assume that your unit ordered 14 staplers at a total cost of $30.20, and each stapler cost the same.
The cost of one stapler was MOST NEARLY

    A. $1.02   B. $1.61   C. $2.16   D. $2.26

24._____

25. Assume that you are responsible for counting and recording licensing fees collected by your department. On a particular day, your department collected in fees 40 checks in the amount of $6 each, 80 checks in the amount of $4 each, 45 twenty dollar bills, 30 ten dollar bills, 42 five dollar bills, and 186 one dollar bills.
The TOTAL amount in fees collected on that day was

    A. $1,406   B. $1,706   C. $2,156   D. $2,356

25._____

26. Assume that you are responsible for your agency's petty cash fund. During the month of February, you pay out 7 $2.00 subway fares and one taxi fare for $10.85. You pay out nothing else from the fund. At the end of February, you count the money left in the fund and find 3 one dollar bills, 4 quarters, 5 dimes, and 4 nickels. The amount of money you had available in the petty cash fund at the BEGINNING of February was

    A. $4.70   B. $16.35   C. $24.85   D. $29.55

26._____

27. You overhear your supervisor criticize a co-worker for handling equipment in an unsafe way. You feel that the criticism may be unfair.
Of the following, it would be BEST for you to

    A. take your co-worker aside and tell her how you feel about your supervisor's comments
    B. interrupt the discussion and defend your co-worker to your supervisor
    C. continue working as if you had not overheard the discussion
    D. make a list of other workers who have violated safety rules and give it to your supervisor

27._____

28. Assume that you have been assigned to work on a long-term project with an employee who is known for being uncooperative.
In beginning to work with this employee, it would be LEAST desirable for you to

    A. understand why the person is uncooperative
    B. act in a calm manner rather than an emotional manner
    C. be appreciative of the co-worker's work
    D. report the co-worker's lack of cooperation to your supervisor

28._____

29. Assume that you are assigned to sell tickets at a city-owned ice skating rink. An adult ticket costs $4.50, and a children's ticket costs $2.25. At the end of a day, you find that you have sold 36 adult tickets and 80 children's tickets.
The TOTAL amount of money you collected for that day was

    A. $244.80   B. $318.00   C. $342.00   D. $348.00

29._____

30. If each office worker files 487 index cards in one hour, how many cards can 26 office workers file in one hour?

    A. 10,662   B. 12,175   C. 12,662   D. 14,266

30._____

KEY (CORRECT ANSWERS)

1.	D	16.	C
2.	B	17.	C
3.	A	18.	C
4.	D	19.	A
5.	A	20.	B
6.	A	21.	B
7.	C	22.	A
8.	B	23.	C
9.	A	24.	C
10.	C	25.	C
11.	C	26.	D
12.	D	27.	C
13.	A	28.	D
14.	C	29.	C
15.	D	30.	C

EXAMINATION SECTION
TEST 1

DIRECTIONS: Each question or incomplete statement is followed by several suggested answers or completions. Select the one that BEST answers the question or completes the statement. *PRINT THE LETTER OF THE CORRECT ANSWER IN THE SPACE AT THE RIGHT.*

Questions 1-10.

WORD MEANING

DIRECTIONS: Each question from 1 to 10 contains a word in capitals followed by four suggested meanings of the word. For each question, choose the best meaning. *PRINT THE LETTER OF THE CORRECT ANSWER IN THE SPACE AT THE RIGHT.*

1. ACCURATE   1._____
    A. correct   B. useful   C. afraid   D. careless

2. ALTER   2._____
    A. copy   B. change   C. report   D. agree

3. DOCUMENT   3._____
    A. outline   B. agreement   C. blueprint   D. record

4. INDICATE   4._____
    A. listen   B. show   C. guess   D. try

5. INVENTORY   5._____
    A. custom   B. discovery   C. warning   D. list

6. ISSUE   6._____
    A. annoy   B. use up   C. give out   D. gain

7. NOTIFY   7._____
    A. inform   B. promise   C. approve   D. strengthen

8. ROUTINE   8._____
    A. path   B. mistake   C. habit   D. journey

9. TERMINATE   9._____
    A. rest   B. start   C. deny   D. end

10. TRANSMIT   10._____
    A. put in   B. send   C. stop   D. go across

Questions 11-15.

READING COMPREHENSION

DIRECTIONS: Questions 11 through 15 test how well you understand what you read. It will be necessary for you to read carefully because your answers to these questions should be based ONLY on the information given in the following paragraphs.

The recipient gains an impression of a typewritten letter before he begins to read the message. Pastors which provide for a good first impression include margins and spacing that are visually pleasing, formal parts of the letter which are correctly placed according to the style of the letter, copy which is free of obvious erasures and over-strikes, and transcript that is even and clear. The problem for the typist is that of how to produce that first, positive impression of her work.

There are several general rules which a typist can follow when she wishes to prepare a properly spaced letter on a sheet of letter-head. Ordinarily, the width of a letter should not be less than four inches nor more than six inches. The side margins should also have a desirable relation to the bottom margin and the space between the letterhead and the body of the letter. Usually the most appealing arrangement is when the side margins are even and the bottom margin is slightly wider than the side margins. In some offices, however, standard line length is used for all business letters, and the secretary then varies the spacing between the date line and the inside address according to the length of the letter.

11.   The BEST title for the above paragraphs would be: 11.____

    A.   Writing Office Letters
    B.   Making Good First Impressions
    C.   Judging Well-Typed Letters
    D.   Good Placing and Spacing for Office Letters

12.   According to the above paragraphs, which of the following might be considered the way   12.____
    in which people very quickly judge the quality of work which has been typed? By

    A.   measuring the margins to see if they are correct
    B.   looking at the spacing and cleanliness of the typescript
    C.   scanning the body of the letter for meaning
    D.   reading the date line and address for errors

13.   What, according to the above paragraphs, would be definitely UNDESIRABLE as the   13.____
    average line length of a typed letter?

    A.   4"   B.   5"   C.   6"   D.   7"

14.   According to the above paragraphs, when the line length is kept standard, the secretary   14.____

    A.   does not have to vary the spacing at all since this also is standard
    B.   adjusts the spacing between the date line and inside address for different lengths of letters
    C.   uses the longest line as a guideline for spacing between the date line and inside address
    D.   varies the number of spaces between the lines

15. According to the above paragraphs, side margins are MOST pleasing when they   15._____

    A.   are even and somewhat smaller than the bottom margin
    B.   are slightly wider than the bottom margin
    C.   vary with the length of the letter
    D.   are figured independently from the letterhead and the body of the letter

Questions 16-20.

CODING

DIRECTIONS:

Name of Applicant	H	A	N	G	S	B	R	U	K	E
Test Code	c	o	m	p	l	e	x	i	t	y
File Number	0	1	2	3	4	5	6	7	8	9

Assume that each of the above capital letters is the first letter of the name of an Applicant, that the small letter directly beneath each capital letter is the test code for the Applicant, and that the number directly beneath each code letter is the file number for the Applicant.

In each of the following Questions 16 through 20, the test code letters and the file numbers in Columns 2 and 3 should correspond to the capital letters in Column 1. For each question, look at each column carefully and mark your answer as follows:

    If there is an error only in Column 2, mark your
    answer A.
    If there is an error only in Column 3, mark your
    answer B.
    If there is an error in both Columns 2 and 3, mark
    your answer C.
    If both Columns 2 and 3 are correct, mark your
    answer D.

The following sample question is given to help you understand the procedure.

SAMPLE QUESTION

Column 1	Column 2	Column 3
AKEHN	otyci	18902

In Column 2, the final test code letter *i.* should be *m.* Column 3 is correctly coded to Column 1. Since there is an error only in Column 2, the answer is A.

	Column 1	Column 2	Column 3	
16.	NEKKU	mytti	29987	16._____
17.	KRAEB	txyle	86095	17._____
18.	ENAUK	ymoit	92178	18._____
19.	REANA	xeomo	69121	19._____
20.	EKHSE	ytcxy	97049	20._____

Questions 21-30.

ARITHMETICAL REASONING

21. If a secretary answered 28 phone calls and typed the addresses for 112 credit state-
    ments in one morning, what is the ratio of phone calls answered to credit statements
    typed for that period of time?

    A. 1:4   B. 1:7   C. 2:3   D. 3:5

21.____

22. According to a suggested filing system, no more than 10 folders should be filed behind
    any one file guide and from 15 to 25 file guides should be used in each file drawer for
    easy finding and filing.
    The maximum number of folders that a five-drawer file cabinet can hold to allow easy
    finding and filing is

    A. 550   B. 750   C. 1,100   D. 1,250

22.____

23. An employee had a starting salary of $25,804. He received a salary increase at the end
    of each year, and at the end of the seventh year his salary was $33,476.
    What was his average annual increase in salary over these seven years?

    A. $1,020   B. $1,076   C. $1,096   D. $1,144

23.____

24. The 55 typists and 28 senior clerks in a certain city agency were paid a total of
    $1,943,200 in salaries last year.
    If the average annual salary of a typist was $22,400 the average annual salary of a
    senior clerk was

    A. $25,400   B. $26,600   C. $26,800   D. $27,000

24.____

25. A typist has been given a three page report to type. She has finished typing the first two
    pages. The first page has 283 words, and the second page has 366 words.
    If the total report consists of 954 words, how many words will she have to type on the
    third page of the report?

    A. 202   B. 287   C. 305   D. 313

25.____

26. In one day, Clerk A processed 30% more forms than Clerk B, and Clerk C processed li
    times as many forms as Clerk A. If Clerk B processed 40 forms, how many more forms
    were processed by Clerk C than Clerk B?

    A. 12   B. 13   C. 21   D. 25

26.____

27. A clerk who earns a gross salary of $452 every two weeks has the following deductions
    taken from her paycheck:
    15% for City, State, Federal taxes; 2 1/2% for Social Security; $1.30 for health insur-
    ance; and $6.00 for union dues. The amount of her take-home pay is

    A. $256.20   B. $312.40   C. $331.60   D. $365.60

27.____

28. In 2005, a city agency spent $2,000 to buy pencils at a cost of $5.00 a dozen.
    If the agency used 3/4 of these pencils in 2005 and used the same number of pencils
    in 2006, how many more pencils did it have to buy to have enough pencils for all of
    2006?

    A. 1,200   B. 2,400   C. 3,600   D. 4,800

28.____

29. A clerk who worked in Agency X earned the following salaries: $20,140 the first year, $21,000 the second year, and $21,920 the third year. Another clerk who worked in Agency Y for three years earned $21,100 a year for two years and $21,448 the third year. The difference between the average salaries received by both clerks over a three-year period is   29.____

    A. $196   B. $204   C. $348   D. $564

30. An employee who works over 40 hours in any week receives overtime payment for the extra hours at time and one-half (1 1/2 times) his hourly rate of pay. An employee who earns $13.60 an hour works a total of 45 hours during a certain week.
His total pay for that week would be   30.____

    A. $564.40   B. $612.00   C. $646.00   D. $812.00

Questions 31-35.

RELATED INFORMATION

31. To tell a newly-employed clerk to fill a top drawer of a four-drawer cabinet with heavy folders which will be often used and to keep lower drawers only partly filled is   31.____

    A. *good,* because a tall person would have to bend unnecessarily if he had to use a lower drawer
    B. *bad,* because the file cabinet may tip over when the top drawer is opened
    C. *good,* because it is the most easily reachable drawer for the average person
    D. *bad,* because a person bending down at another drawer may accidentally bang his head on the bottom of the drawer when he straightens up

32. If a senior typist or senior clerk has requisitioned a *ream* of paper in order to duplicate a single page office announcement, how many announcements can be printed from the one package of paper?   32.____

    A. 200   B. 500   C. 700   D. 1,000

33. Your supervisor has asked you to locate a telephone number for an attorney named Jones, whose office is located at 311 Broadway, and whose name is not already listed in your files.
The BEST method for finding the number would be for you to   33.____

    A. call the information operator and have her get it for you
    B. look in the alphabetical directory (white pages) under the name Jones at 311 Broadway
    C. refer to the heading Attorney in the yellow pages for the name Jones at 311 Broadway
    D. ask your supervisor who referred her to Mr. Jones, then call that person for the number

34. An example of material that should NOT be sent by first class mail is a   34.____

    A. email copy of a letter   B. post card
    C. business reply card   D. large catalogue

35. In the operations of a government agency, a voucher is ORDINARILY used to
    A. refer someone to the agency for a position or assignment
    B. certify that an agency's records of financial trans-actions are accurate
    C. order payment from agency funds of a stated amount to an individual
    D. enter a statement of official opinion in the records of the agency

35._____

Questions 36-40.

ENGLISH USAGE

DIRECTIONS: Each question from 36 through 40 contains a sentence. Read each sentence carefully to decide whether it is correct. Then, in the space at the right, mark your answer:

(A) if the sentence is incorrect because of bad grammar or sentence structure

(B) if the sentence is incorrect because of bad punctuation

(C) if the sentence is incorrect because of bad capitalization

(D) if the sentence is correct

Each incorrect sentence has only one type of error. Consider a sentence correct if it has no errors, although there may be other correct ways of saying the same thing.

SAMPLE QUESTION I: One of our clerks were promoted yesterday.

The subject of this sentence is *one*, so the verb should be *was promoted* instead of *were promoted*. Since the sentence is incorrect because of bad grammar, the answer to Sample Question I is (A).

SAMPLE QUESTION II: Between you and me, I would prefer not going there.

Since this sentence is correct, the answer to Sample Question II is (D).

36. The National alliance of Businessmen is trying to persuade private businesses to hire youth in the summertime.

36._____

37. The supervisor who is on vacation, is in charge of processing vouchers.

37._____

38. The activity of the committee at its conferences is always stimulating.

38._____

39. After checking the addresses again, the letters went to the mailroom.

39._____

40. The director, as well as the employees, are interested in sharing the dividends.

40._____

36

Questions 41-45.

FILING

DIRECTIONS: Each question from 41 through 45 contains four names. For each question, choose the name that should be FIRST if the four names are to be arranged in alphabeti-cal order in accordance with the Rules for Alphabetical Filing given below. Read these rules carefully. Then, for each question, indicate in the space at the right the letter before the name that should be FIRST in alphabet-ical order.

RULES FOR ALPHABETICAL FILING

Names of People

(1)   The names of people are filed in strict alphabetical order, first according to the last name, then according to first name or initial, and finally according to middle name or initial. FOR EXAMPLE: George Allen comes before Edward Bell, and Leonard P. Reston comes before Lucille B. Reston.

(2)   When last names are the same, FOR EXAMPLE, A. Green and Agnes Green, the one with the initial comes before the one with the name written out when the first initials are identical.

(3)   When first and last names are alike and the middle name is given, FOR EXAMPLE, John David Doe and John Devoe Doe, the names should be filed in the alphabetical order of the middle names.

(4)   When first and last names are the same, a name without a middle initial comes before one with a middle name or initial. FOR EXAMPLE, John Doe comes before both John A. Doe and John Alan Doe.

(5)   When first and last names are the same, a name with a middle initial comes before one with a middle name beginning with the same initial. FOR EXAMPLE: Jack R. Hertz comes before Jack Richard Hertz.

(6)   Prefixes such as De, O', Mac, Mc, and Van are filed as written and are treated as part of the names to which they are connected. FOR EXAMPLE: Robert O'Dea is filed before David Olsen.

(7)   Abbreviated names are treated as if they were spelled out. FOR EXAMPLE: Chas. is filed as Charles and Thos. is filed as Thomas.

(8)   Titles and designations such as Dr., Mr., and Prof, are disregarded in filing.

Names of Organizations

(1)   The names of business organizations are filed according to the order in which each word in the name appears. When an organization name bears the name of a person, it is filed according to the rules for filing names of people as given above. FOR EXAMPLE: William Smith Service Co. comes before Television Distributors, Inc.

(2) *Where bureau, board, office, or department appears as the first part of the title of a governmental agency, that agency should be filed under the word in the title expressing the chief function of the agency. FOR EXAMPLE: Bureau of the Budget would be filed as if written Budget, (Bureau of the). The Department of Personnel would be filed as if written Personnel, (Department of).*

(3) *When the following words are part of an organization, they are disregarded: the, of, and.*

(4) *When there are numbers in a name, they are treated as if they were spelled out. FOR EXAMPLE: 10th Street Bootery is filed as Tenth Street Bootery.*

SAMPLE QUESTION: A. Jane Earl   (2)
                   B. James A. Earle   (4)
                   C. James Earl   (1)
                   D. J. Earle   (3)

The numbers in parentheses show the proper alphabetical order in which these names should be filed. Since the name that should be filed FIRST is James Earl, the answer to the Sample Question is (C).

41.   A. Majorca Leather Goods   41._____
      B. Robert Maiorca and Sons
      C. Maintenance Management Corp.
      D. Majestic Carpet Mills

42.   A. Municipal Telephone Service   42._____
      B. Municipal Reference Library
      C. Municipal Credit Union
      D. Municipal Broadcasting System

43.   A. Robert B. Pierce   B. R. Bruce Pierce   43._____
      C. Ronald Pierce   D. Robert Bruce Pierce

44.   A. Four Seasons Sports Club B. 14th. St. Shopping Center   44._____
      C. Forty Thieves Restaurant D. 42nd St. Theaters

45.   A. Franco Franceschini   B. Amos Franchini   45._____
      C. Sandra Franceschia   D. Lilie Franchinesca

Questions 46-50.

SPELLING

DIRECTIONS: In each question, one of the words is misspelled. Select the letter of the misspelled word. *PRINT THE LETTER OF THE CORRECT ANSWER IN THE SPACE AT THE RIGHT.*

46.   A. option   B. extradite   46._____
      C. comparitive   D. jealousy

47.   A. handicaped   B. assurance   47._____
      C. sympathy   D. speech

48.	A. recommend	B. carraige	48.____
	C. disapprove	D. independent	

49.	A. ingenuity	B. tenet (opinion)	49.____
	C. uncanny	D. intrigueing	

50.	A. arduous	B. hideous	50.____
	C. iervant	D. companies	

KEY (CORRECT ANSWERS)

1. A	11. D	21. A	31. B	41. C
2. B	12. B	22. D	32. B	42. D
3. D	13. D	23. C	33. C	43. B
4. B	14. B	24. A	34. D	44. D
5. D	15. A	25. C	35. C	45. C
6. C	16. B	26. D	36. C	46. C
7. A	17. C	27. D	37. B	47. A
8. C	18. D	28. B	38. D	48. B
9. D	19. A	29. A	39. A	49. D
10. B	20. C	30. C	40. A	50. C'

EXAMINATION SECTION
TEST 1

DIRECTIONS: Each question or incomplete statement is followed by several suggested answers or completions. Select the one that BEST answers the question or completes the statement. *PRINT THE LETTER OF THE CORRECT ANSWER IN THE SPACE AT THE RIGHT.*

Questions 1-4.

DIRECTIONS: Answer Questions 1 through 4 SOLELY on the basis of the following passage.

Job analysis combined with performance appraisal is an excellent method of determining training needs of individuals. The steps in this method are to determine the specific duties of the job, to evaluate the adequacy with which the employee performs each of these duties, and finally to determine what significant improvements can be made by training.

The list of duties can be obtained in a number of ways: asking the employee, asking the supervisor, observing the employee, etc. Adequacy of performance can be estimated by the employee, but the supervisor's evaluation must also be obtained. This evaluation will usually be based on observation.

What does the supervisor observe? The employee, while he is working; the employee's work relationships; the ease, speed, and sureness of the employee's actions; the way he applies himself to the job; the accuracy and amount of completed work; its conformity with established procedures and standards; the appearance of the work; the soundness of judgment it shows; and, finally, signs of good or poor communication, understanding, and cooperation among employees.

Such observation is a normal and inseparable part of the everyday job of supervision. Systematically, recorded, evaluated, and summarized, it highlights both general and individual training needs.

1. According to the passage, job analysis may be used by the supervisor in   1.____

   A. increasing his own understanding of tasks performed in his unit
   B. increasing efficiency of communication within the organization
   C. assisting personnel experts in the classification of positions
   D. determining in which areas an employee needs more instruction

2. According to the passage, the FIRST step in determining the training needs of employ-   2.____
   ees is to

   A. locate the significant improvements that can be made by training
   B. determine the specific duties required in a job
   C. evaluate the employee's performance
   D. motivate the employee to want to improve himself

3. On the basis of the above passage, which of the following is the BEST way for a supervi-   3.____
   sor to determine the adequacy of employee performance?

   A. Check the accuracy and amount of completed work
   B. Ask the training officer
   C. Observe all aspects of the employee's work
   D. Obtain the employee's own estimate

4. Which of the following is NOT mentioned by the passage as a factor to be taken into consideration in judging the adequacy of employee performance?

    A. Accuracy of completed work
    B. Appearance of completed work
    C. Cooperation among employees
    D. Attitude of the employee toward his supervisor

4.____

5. In indexing names of business firms and other organizations, ONE of the rules to be followed is:

    A. The word *and* is considered an indexing unit
    B. When a firm name includes the full name of a person who is not well-known, the
   person's first name is considered as the first indexing unit
    C. Usually the units in a firm name are indexed in the order in which they are written
    D. When a firm's name is made up of single letters (such as ABC Corp.), the letters
   taken together are considered more than one indexing unit

5.____

6. Assume that people often come to your office with complaints of errors in your agency's
   handling of their clients. The employees in your office have the job of listening to these
   complaints and investigating them. One day, when it is almost closing time, a person
   comes into your office, apparently very angry, and demands that you take care of his
   complaint at once.
   Your IMMEDIATE reaction should be to

    A. suggest that he return the following day
    B. find out his name and the nature of his complaint
    C. tell him to write a letter
    D. call over your superior

6.____

7. Assume that part of your job is to notify people concerning whether their applications for
   a certain program have been approved or disapproved. However, you do not actually
   make the decision on approval or disapproval. One day, you answer a telephone call
   from a woman who states that she has not yet received any word on her application. She
   goes on to tell you her qualifications for the program. From what she has said, you know
   that persons with such qualifications are usually approved.
   Of the following, which one is the BEST thing for you to say to her?

    A. "You probably will be accepted, but wait until you receive a letter before trying to
   join the program."
    B. "Since you seem well qualified, I am sure that your application will be approved."
    C. "If you can write us a letter emphasizing your qualifications, it may speed up the
   process."
    D. "You will be notified of the results of your application as soon as a decision has
   been made."

7.____

8. Suppose that one of your duties includes answering specific telephone inquiries. Your
   superior refers a call to you from an irate person who claims that your agency is ineffi-
   cient and is wasting taxpayers' money.
   Of the following, the BEST way to handle such a call is to

    A. listen briefly and then hang up without answering
    B. note the caller's comments and tell him that you will transmit them to your superiors

8.____

C. connect the caller with the head of your agency
D. discuss your own opinions with the caller

9. An employee has been assigned to open her division head's mail and place it on his desk. One day, the employee opens a letter which she then notices is marked *Personal.* Of the following, the BEST action for her to take is to   9.____

A. write *Personal* on the letter and staple the envelope to the back of the letter
B. ignore the matter and treat the letter the same way as the others
C. give it to another division head to hold until her own division head comes into the office
D. leave the letter in the envelope and write *Sorry opened by mistake* on the envelope and initial it

Questions 10-14.

DIRECTIONS: Questions 10 through 14 each consist of a quotation which contains one word that is incorrectly used because it is not in keeping with the meaning that the quotation is evidently intended to convey. Of the words underlined in each quotation, determine which word is incorrectly used. Then select from among the words lettered A, B, C, and D the word which, when substituted for the incorrectly used word, would BEST help to convey the meaning of the quotation. (Do NOT indicate a change for an underlined word unless the underlined word is incorrectly used.)

10. Unless reasonable managerial supervision is <u>exercised</u> over office supplies, it is certain that there will be extravagance, <u>rejected</u> items out of stock, <u>excessive</u> prices paid for certain items, and <u>obsolete</u> material in the stockroom.   10.____

A. overlooked
C. needed
B. immoderate
D. instituted

11. Since <u>office</u> supplies are in such <u>common</u> use, an attitude of indifference about their handling is not <u>unusual</u>. Their importance is often recognized only when they are <u>utilized</u> or out of stock, for office employees must have proper supplies if maximum productivity is to be <u>attained</u>.   11.____

A. plentiful
C. reduced
B. unavailable
D. expected

12. Anyone <u>effected</u> by paperwork, <u>interested</u> in or engaged in office work, or desiring to improve <u>informational</u> activities can find materials <u>keyed</u> to his needs.   12.____

A. attentive   B. available   C. affected   D. ambitious

13. Information is <u>homogeneous</u> and must therefore be properly classified so that each type may be <u>employed</u> in ways <u>appropriate</u> to its <u>own peculiar</u> properties.   13.____

A. apparent
C. consistent
B. heterogeneous
D. idiosyncratic

14. <u>Intellectual</u> training may seem a <u>formidable</u> phrase, but it means nothing more than the <u>deliberate</u> cultivation of the ability to think, and there is no <u>dark</u> contrast between the intellectual and the practical.   14.____

A. subjective   B. objective
C. sharp   D. vocational

15. The MOST important reason for having a filing system is to   15._____

     A. get papers out of the way
     B. have a record of everything that has happened
     C. retain information to justify your actions
     D. enable rapid retrieval of information

16. The system of filing which is used MOST frequently is called _____ filing.   16._____

     A. alphabetic   B. alphanumeric
     C. geographic   D. numeric

17. One of the clerks under your supervision has been telephoning frequently to tell you that   17._____
he was taking the day off. Unless there is a real need for it, taking leave which is not
scheduled is frowned upon because it upsets the work schedule.
Under these circumstances, which of the following reasons for taking the day off is
MOST acceptable?

     A. "I can't work when my arthritis bothers me."
     B. "I've been pressured with work from my night job and needed the extra time to
        catch up."
     C. "My family just moved to a new house, and I needed the time to start the repairs."
     D. "Work here has not been challenging, and I've been looking for another job."

18. One of the employees under your supervision, previously a very satisfactory worker, has   18._____
begun arriving late one or two mornings each week. No explanation has been offered for
this change. You call her to your office for a conference. As you are explaining the purpose of the conference and your need to understand this sudden lateness problem, she
becomes angry and states that you have no right to question her.
Of the following, the BEST course of action for you to take at this point is to

     A. inform her in your most authoritarian tone that you are the supervisor and that you
        have every right to question her
     B. end the conference and advise the employee that you will have no further discus-
        sion with her until she controls her temper
     C. remain calm, try to calm her down, and when she has quieted, explain the reasons
        for your questions and the need for answers
     D. hold your temper; when she has calmed down, tell her that you will not have a
        tardy worker in your unit and will have her transferred at once

19. Assume that, in the branch of the agency for which you work, you are the only clerical   19._____
person on the staff with a supervisory title and, in addition, that you are the office manager. On a particular day when all members of the professional staff are away from the
building attending an important meeting, an urgent call comes through requesting some
confidential information ordinarily released only by professional staff.
Of the following, the MOST reasonable action for you to take is to

     A. decline to give the information because you are not a member of the professional
        staff
     B. offer to call back after you get permission from the agency director at the main
        office

C. advise the caller that you will supply the information as soon as your chief returns
D. supply the information requested and inform your chief when she returns

20. As a supervisor, you are scheduled to attend an important conference with your superior. However, that day you learn that your very capable assistant is ill and unable to come to work. Several highly sensitive tasks are scheduled for completion on this day.
Of the following, the BEST way to handle this situation is to

    20._____

A. tell your supervisor you cannot attend the meeting and ask that it be postponed
B. assign one of your staff to see that the jobs are completed and turned in
C. advise your supervisor of the situation and ask what you should do
D. call the departments for which the work is being done and ask for an extension of time

21. When a decision needs to be made which is likely to affect units other than his own, a supervisor should USUALLY

    21._____

A. make such a decision quickly and then discuss it with his supervisor
B. make such a decision only after careful consultation with his subordinates
C. discuss the problem with his immediate superior before making such a decision
D. have his subordinates arrive at such a decision in conference with the subordinates in the other units

22. Assume that, as a supervisor in Division X, you are training Ms. Y, a new employee, to answer the telephone properly.
You should explain that the BEST way to answer is to pick up the receiver and say:

    22._____

A. "What is your name, please?"
B. "May I help you?"
C. "Ms. Y speaking."
D. "Division X, Ms. Y speaking."

Questions 23-25.

DIRECTIONS: Questions 23 through 25 consist of sentences in which two words are missing. Examine each sentence, and then choose from below it the words which should be inserted in the blank spaces in order to create a coherent and well-written sentence.

23. Human behavior is far _____ variable, and therefore _____ predictable, than that of any other species.

    23._____

A. less; as   B. less; not
C. more; not   D. more; less

24. The _____ limitation of this method is that the results are based _____ a narrow sample.

    24._____

A. chief; with   B. chief; on
C. only; for   D. only; to

25. Although there _____ a standard procedure for handling these problems, each case often has _____ own unique features.

    25._____

A. are; its   B. are; their
C. is; its   D. is; their

KEY (CORRECT ANSWERS)

1.	D		11.	B
2.	B		12.	C
3.	C		13.	B
4.	D		14.	C
5.	C		15.	D
6.	B		16.	A
7.	D		17.	A
8.	B		18.	C
9.	D		19.	B
10.	C		20.	C

21.	C
22.	D
23.	D
24.	B
25.	C

TEST 2

DIRECTIONS: Each question or incomplete statement is followed by several suggested answers or completions. Select the one that BEST answers your question or completes the statement. *PRINT THE LETTER OF THE CORRECT ANSWER IN THE SPACE AT THE RIGHT.*

Questions 1-3.

DIRECTIONS: Questions 1 through 3 each consist of a group of four sentences. Read each sentence carefully, and select the one of the four in each group which represents the BEST English usage for business letters and reports.

1. A. The chairman himself, rather than his aides, hasreviewed the report.   1.____
    B. The chairman himself, rather than his aides, have reviewed the report.
    C. The chairmen, not the aide, has reviewed the report.
    D. The aide, not the chairmen, have reviewed the report.

2. A. Various proposals were submitted but the decision is not been made.   2.____
    B. Various proposals has been submitted but the decision has not been made.
    C. Various proposals were submitted but the decision is not been made.
    D. Various proposals have been submitted but the decision has not been made.

3. A. Everyone were rewarded for his successful attempt.   3.____
    B. They were successful in their attempts and each of them was rewarded.
    C. Each of them are rewarded for their successful attempts.
    D. The reward for their successful attempts were made to each of them.

4. Which of the following is MOST suited to arrangement in chronological order?   4.____

    A. Applications for various types and levels of jobs
    B. Issues of a weekly publication
    C. Weekly time cards for all employees for the week of April 21
    D. Personnel records for all employees

5. Words that are *synonymous* with a given word ALWAYS   5.____

    A. have the same meaning as the given word
    B. have the same pronunciation as the given word
    C. have the opposite meaning of the given word
    D. can be rhymed with the given word

Questions 6-11.

DIRECTIONS: Answer Questions 6 through 11 on the basis of the following chart showing numbers of errors made by four clerks in one work unit for a half-year period.

	Allan	Barry	Cary	David
July	5	4	1	7
Aug.	8	3	9	8
Sept.	7	8	7	5
Oct.	3	6	5	3
Nov .	2	4	4	6
Dec.	5	2	8	4

6. The clerk with the HIGHEST number of errors for the six-month period was

   A. Allan   B. Barry   C. Cary   D. David

    6._____

7. If the number of errors made by Allan in the six months shown represented one-eighth of the total errors made by the unit during the entire year, what was the TOTAL number of errors made by the unit for the year?

   A. 124   B. 180   C. 240   D. 360

    7._____

8. The number of errors made by David in November was what FRACTION of the total errors made in November?

   A. 1/3   B. 1/6   C. 3/8   D. 3/16

    8._____

9. The average number of errors made per month per clerk was MOST NEARLY

   A. 4   B. 5   C. 6   D. 7

    9._____

10. Of the total number of errors made during the six-month period, the percentage made in August was MOST NEARLY

    A. 2%   B. 4%   C. 23%   D. 44%

    10._____

11. If the number of errors in the unit were to decrease in the next six months by 30%, what would be MOST NEARLY the total number of errors for the unit for the next six months?

    A. 87   B. 94   C. 120   D. 137

    11._____

12. The arithmetic mean salary for five employees earning $18,500, $18,300, $18,600, $18,400, and $18,500, respectively, is

    A. $18,450   B. $18,460   C. $18,475   D. $18,500

    12._____

13. Last year, a city department which is responsible for purchasing supplies ordered bond paper in equal quantities from 22 different companies. The price was exactly the same for each company, and the total cost for the 22 orders was $693,113.
Assuming prices did not change during the year, the cost of EACH order was MOST NEARLY

    A. $31,490   B. $31,495   C. $31,500   D. $31,505

    13._____

14. A city agency engaged in repair work uses a small part which the city purchases for 14? each. Assume that, in a certain year, the total expenditure of the city for this part was $700.
How MANY of these parts were purchased that year?

    A. 50   B. 200   C. 2,000   D. 5,000

    14._____

15. The work unit which you supervise is responsible for processing fifteen reports per month.
If your unit has four clerks and the best worker completes 40% of the reports himself, how many reports would each of the other clerks have to complete if they all do an equal number?

   A. 1   B. 2   C. 3   D. 4

15.____

16. Assume that the work unit in which you work has 24 clerks and 18 stenographers.
In order to change the ratio of stenographers to clerks so that there is one stenographer for every four clerks, it would be necessary to REDUCE the number of stenographers by

   A. 3   B. 6   C. 9   D. 12

16.____

17. Assume that your office is responsible for opening and distributing all the mail of the division. After opening a letter, one of your subordinates notices that it states that there should be an enclosure in the envelope. However, there is no enclosure in the envelope. Of the following, the BEST instruction that you can give the clerk is to

   A. call the sender to obtain the enclosure
   B. call the addressee to inform him that the enclosure is missing
   C. note the omission in the margin of the letter
   D. forward the letter without taking any action

17.____

18. While opening the envelope containing official correspondence, you accidentally cut the enclosed letter.
Of the following, the BEST action for you to take is to

   A. leave the material as it is
   B. put it together by using transparent mending tape
   C. keep it together by putting it back in the envelope
   D. keep it together by using paper clips

18.____

19. Suppose your supervisor is on the telephone in his office and an applicant arrives for a scheduled interview with him.
Of the following, the BEST procedure to follow ordinarily is to

   A. informally chat with the applicant in your office until your supervisor has finished his phone conversation
   B. escort him directly into your supervisor's office and have him wait for him there
   C. inform your supervisor of the applicant's arrival and try to make the applicant feel comfortable while waiting
   D. have him hang up his coat and tell him to go directly in to see your supervisor

19.____

20. The length of time that files should be kept is GENERALLY

   A. considered to be seven years
   B. dependent upon how much new material has accumulated in the files
   C. directly proportionate to the number of years the office has been in operation
   D. dependent upon the type and nature of the material in the files

20.____

21. Cross-referencing a document when you file it means

A. making a copy of the document and putting the copy into a related file
B. indicating on the front of the document the name of the person who wrote it, the date it was written, and for what purpose
C. putting a special sheet or card in a related file to indicate where the document is filed
D. indicating on the document where it is to be filed

22. Unnecessary handling and recording of incoming mail could be eliminated by
22._____

A. having the person who opens it initial it
B. indicating on the piece of mail the names of all the individuals who should see it
C. sending all incoming mail to more than one central location
D. making a photocopy of each piece of incoming mail

23. Of the following, the office tasks which lend themselves MOST readily to planning and study are
23._____

A. repetitive, occur in volume, and extend over a period of time
B. cyclical in nature, have small volume, and extend over a short period of time
C. tasks which occur only once in a great while not according to any schedule, and have large volume
D. special tasks which occur only once, regardless of their volume and length of time

24. A good recordkeeping system includes all of the following procedures EXCEPT the
24._____

A. filing of useless records
B. destruction of certain files
C. transferring of records from one type of file to another
D. creation of inactive files

25. Assume that, as a supervisor, you are responsible for orienting and training new employ-ees in your unit. Which of the following can MOST properly be omitted from your discus-sions with a new employee?
25._____

A. The purpose of commonly used office forms
B. Time and leave regulations
C. Procedures for required handling of routine business calls
D. The reason the last employee was fired

KEY (CORRECT ANSWERS)

1.	A		11.	A
2.	D		12.	B
3.	B		13.	D
4.	B		14.	D
5.	A		15.	C
6.	C		16.	D
7.	C		17.	C
8.	C		18.	B
9.	B		19.	C
10.	C		20.	D

21.	C
22.	B
23.	A
24.	A
25.	D

VERBAL & CLERICAL ABILITIES
EXAMINATION SECTION

TEST 1

DIRECTIONS: Read each question carefully. Select the best answer and write the letter
in the answer space at the right.

1. PREVIOUS means most nearly
    A. abandoned
    B. timely
    C. former
    D. successive
    E. younger

1._____

2. CONSENSUS means most nearly
    A. accord
    B. abridgment
    C. presumption
    D. quota
    E. exception

2._____

3. LACONIC means most nearly
    A. slothful
    B. concise
    C. punctual
    D. melancholy
    E. indifferent

3._____

4. TRENCHANT means most nearly
    A. urgent
    B. witty
    C. decisive
    D. sharp
    E. merciless

4._____

5. MANDATORY means most nearly
    A. basic
    B. obligatory
    C. discretionary
    D. discriminatory
    E. advisory

5._____

6. OPTION means most nearly
    A. use
    B. choice
    C. value
    D. blame
    E. rule

6._____

7. INNATE means most nearly
    A. eternal
    B. well-developed
    C. native
    D. prospective
    E. understandable

7._____

8. To CONFINE means most nearly to
    A. restrict
    B. hide
    C. eliminate
    D. punish
    E. ruin

8._____

9. A small crane was used to *raise* the heavy parts.
   Raise means most nearly
    A. drag
    B. unload
    C. deliver
    D. lift
    E. guide

9._____

10. The reports were *consolidated* by the secretary.
   Consolidated means most nearly
    A. combined
    B. concluded
    C. distributed
    D. protected
    E. weighed

10._____

11. CROWD is related to PERSONS as FLEET is related to
    A. guns
    B. officers
    C. navy
    D. expedition
    E. ships

11._____

12. SPEEDOMETER is related to POINTER as WATCH is related to
    A. case
    B. hands
    C. dial
    D. numerals
    E. band

12._____

13. PLUMBER is related to WRENCH as PAINTER is related to
    A. brush
    B. pipe
    C. shop
    D. hammer
    E. painting

13._____

14. BODY is related to FOOD as ENGINE is related to   14._____
    A. wheels
    B. smoke
    C. motion
    D. fuel
    E. conductor

15. ABUNDANT is related to CHEAP as SCARCE is related to   15._____
    A. ample
    B. inexpensive
    C. costly
    D. unobtainable
    E. frugal

Reading

16. "One type of advertising on which it is difficult to calculate the return is the radio   16._____
program, offered by so many industries today. The chief return of radio
advertising is goodwill, which industries consider so valuable that they spend
vast sums of money to obtain it."

The quotation BEST supports the statement that radio advertising by industries
    A. is more expensive than other advertising
    B. has its chief value in creating goodwill
    C. is used by all large industries
    D. is of little value
    E. is the most valuable form of advertising

17. "Just as the procedure of a collection department must be clear-cut and definite,   17._____
the steps being taken with the sureness of a skilled chess player, so the various
paragraphs of a collection letter must show clear organization, giving evidence of
a mind that, from the beginning, has had a specific end in view."

The quotation BEST supports the statement that a collection letter should always
    A. show a spirit of sportsmanship
    B. be divided into several paragraphs
    C. express confidence in the debtor
    D. be brief, but courteous
    E. be carefully planned

18. "One of the primary steps in the development of management in any enterprise is proper organization. After the business has been conceived and the broad policies that are to be pursued have been established, before any operating methods may be devised, at least a skeleton organization must be developed."

The quotation BEST supports the statement that, in industry, some kind of organization is necessary in order that
    A. the type of enterprise may be decided upon
    B. policies may be established
    C. routine work may be planned
    D. capital may be invested
    E. a manager may be selected

19. "The division of labor into the categories of physical and mental labor is not strictly accurate. The labor of even the most unskilled workman calls for the exercise of certain mental qualities, like attention, memory, and prudence; and on the other hand, the intellectual effort of the great captains of industry is associated with a certain amount of waste of tissue."

19

The quotation BEST supports the statement that
    A. There is no real distinction between physical and mental labor.
    B. Manual labor does not call for so great a waste of tissue as intellectual effort does.
    C. The exercise of mental qualities remains the most important feature of labor.
    D. Physical and mental labor require use of the same mental qualities.
    E. The difference between various forms of labor is one of degree.

20. "Proper supervision of play involves a recognition of the fact that a happy childhood through play is essential to a child's normal growth and personal development. Self-discipline and right conduct are natural results of a situation in which a child engages in activities of absorbing interest under wise guidance."

The quotation BEST supports the statement that the proper supervision of play
    A. is of greater benefit to some children than to others
    B. has as its chief purpose training for self-discipline
    C. helps a child to obtain satisfactory results from his recreation
    D. is less essential as a child becomes more absorbed in his play
    E. provides for the natural development of differences in personalities

21. "Alertness and attentiveness are qualities essential for success as a receptionist. The work the receptionist performs often takes careful attention under conditions of stress."

The quotation BEST supports the statement that a receptionist
    A. always works under great strain
    B. cannot be successful unless she memorizes many extensions
    C. must be trained before she can render good service
    D. must be able to work under difficulties
    E. performs more difficult work than do clerical office workers

22. "Probably few people realize, as they drive on a concrete road, that steel is used to keep the surface flat and even, in spite of the weight of busses and trucks. Steel bars, deeply imbedded in the concrete, provide sinews to take the stresses so that they cannot crack the slab or make it wavy."

22._____

The quotation BEST supports the statement that a concrete road
   A. is expensive to build
   B. usually cracks under heavy weights
   C. is used exclusively for heavy traffic
   D. is reinforced with other material

23. "Whenever two groups of people whose interests at the moment conflict meet to discuss a solution of that conflict, there is laid the basis for an interchange of facts and ideas which increases the total range of knowledge of both parties and tends to break down the barrier which their restricted field of information has helped to create."

23._____

The quotation BEST supports the statement that conflicts between two parties may be brought closer to a settlement through
   A. frank acknowledgment of error
   B. the exchange of accusations
   C. gaining a wider knowledge of facts
   D. submitting the dispute to an impartial judge
   E. limiting discussion to plans acceptable to both groups

24. "What constitutes skill in any line of work is not always easy to determine; economy of time must be carefully distinguished from economy of energy, as the quickest method may require the greatest expenditure of muscular effort, and may not be essential or at all desirable."

24._____

The quotation BEST supports the statement that
   A. energy and time cannot both be conserved in the performing of a single task
   B. the most efficiently executed task is not always the one done in the shortest time
   C. if a task requires muscular energy, it is not being performed economically
   D. skill in performing a task should not be acquired at the expense of time
   E. a task is well done when it is performed in the shortest time

25. "The secretarial profession is a very old one and has increased in importance with the passage of time. In modern times, the vast expansion of business and industry has greatly increased the need and opportunities for secretaries, and for the first time in history their number has become large."

25._____

The quotation BEST supports the statement that the secretarial profession
   A. is older than business and industry
   B. did not exist in ancient times
   C. has greatly increased in size
   D. demands higher training than it did formerly
   E. is not in high enough demand

26. "It is difficult to distinguish between bookkeeping and accounting. In attempts to do so, bookkeeping is called the art, and accounting the science, of recording business transactions. Bookkeeping gives the history of the business in a systematic manner; and accounting classifies, analyzes, and interprets the facts thus recorded."

    26._____

    The quotation BEST supports the statement that
    A. accounting is less systematic than bookkeeping
    B. accounting and bookkeeping are closely related
    C. bookkeeping and accounting cannot be distinguished from one another
    D. bookkeeping has been superseded by accounting
    E. bookkeeping is more practical than accounting

Spelling. Find which choice is spelled correctly and mark the letter in the space at the right.

27. A. athalete
    B. athlete
    C. athelete
    D. none of the above

    27._____

28. A. predesessor
    B. predecesar
    C. predecesser
    D. none of the above

    28._____

29. A. occasion
    B. occasion
    C. ocassion
    D. none of the above

    29._____

30. A. Mobile, Ala.
    B. Brocton, Mass.
    C. Yeork, Pa.
    D. Sou Falls, S. Dak.
    E. none of the above

    30._____

31. A. Brookelin, N.Y.
    B. Alambra, Calif.
    C. Attlanta, Ga.
    D. Joplinn, Mo.
    E. none of the above

    31._____

Grammar. Decide which sentence is preferable with respect to grammar and usage suitable for a formal letter or report and mark the letter in the space at the right.

32. A. They do not ordinarily present these kind of reports in detail like this.
    B. Reports like this is not generally given in such great detail.
    C. A report of this kind is not hardly ever given in such detail as this one.
    D. This report is more detailed than what such reports ordinarily are.
    E. A report of this kind is not ordinarily presented in such detail as this one.

32._____

33. A. No other city anywheres in the State has grown so fast as this city.
    B. This city has grown more rapidly than any other city in the State.
    C. No other city in the State has grown as fast or faster than this city.
    D. The growth of this city has been more rapid than any other city in the State.
    E. This city has grown the fastest of all the others in the State.

33._____

34. A. The manager told Mr. Jones and I that we were expected to attend the meeting.
    B. Mr. Jones and I were told by the manager that is was necessary for both of us to have attended the meeting.
    C. In his talk with Mr. Jones and I, the manager explained that our attendance at the meeting was expected.
    D. The manager said that he expected Mr. Jones and me to attend the meeting.
    E. The manager explained to Mr. Jones and myself that it was necessary for us to be present at the meeting.

34._____

35. A. Neither the editor nor his assistant will approve that type of report.
    B. That kind of a report is not acceptable to either the editor or his assistant.
    C. A report of that kind is acceptable to neither the editor or his assistant.
    D. Both the editor and his assistant are sort of unwilling to approve a report like that.
    E. Neither the editor nor his assistant are willing to approve that type of report.

35._____

36. A. I haven't no report on your call yet.
    B. I had ought to receive a report on your call soon.
    C. Can I ring you when I have a report on your call?
    D. Do you want for me to ring as soon as I receive a report on your call?
    E. I do not have any report on your call yet.

36._____

37. A. Our activities this month have been as interesting, if not more interesting than those of any other month this year.
    B. Our activities this year have seldom ever been as interesting as they have been this month.
    C. Our activities this month have been more interesting than those of any other month this year.
    D. Our activities this month have been more interesting, or at least as interesting as those of any month this year.
    E. This month's activities have been more interesting than any previous month during the year.

37._____

38. A. If properly addressed, the letter will reach my mother and I.
    B. The letter had been addressed to myself and my mother.
    C. I believe the letter was addressed to either my mother or I.
    D. My mother's name, as well as mine, was on the letter.
    E. The letter will get to my mother and myself if properly addressed.

38._____

39. A. Most all these statements have been supported by persons who are reliable and can be depended upon.
    B. The persons which have guaranteed these statements are reliable.
    C. Reliable persons guarantee the facts with regards to the truth of these statements.
    D. These statements can be depended on, for their truth has been guaranteed by reliable persons.
    E. The persons who guarantee these statements are very much reliable.

39._____

40. A. Brown's & Company employees have recently received increases in salary.
    B. Brown.& Company recently increased the salaries of all its employees.
    C. Recently Brown & Company has increased their employees' salaries.
    D. Brown & Company have recently increased the salaries of all its employees.
    E. Brown & Company employees have all been increased in salary.

40._____

KEY (CORRECT ANSWERS)

1.	C	16.	B	31.	E
2.	A	17.	E	32.	E
3.	B	18.	C	33.	B
4.	D	19.	E	34.	D
5.	B	20.	C	35.	A
6.	B	21.	D	36.	E
7.	C	22.	D	37.	C
8.	A	23.	C	38.	D
9.	D	24.	B	39.	D
10.	A	25.	C	40.	B
11.	E	26.	B		
12.	B	27.	B		
13.	A	28.	D		
14.	D	29.	B		
15.	C	30.	A		

TEST 2

Questions 1-4.

DIRECTIONS: Below are underlined names, followed by alphabetical names. The spaces between names are lettered A, B, C, D, and E. Decide in which space the underlined name belongs and write the letter in the answer space at right.

1. <u>Kessler, Neilson</u>   1._____

    A)_____

       Kessel, Oscar

    B)_____

       Kessinger, D.J.

    C)_____

       Kessler, Karl

    D)_____

       Kessner, Lewis

    E)_____

2. <u>Jones, Jane</u>   2._____

    A)_____

       Goodyear, G.L.

    B)_____

       Haddon, Harry

    C)_____

       Jackson, Mary

    D)_____

       Jenkins, William

    E)_____

3. <u>Olsen, C.C.</u>

    A)_____

       Olsen, C.A.

    B)_____

       Olsen, C.D.

    C)_____

       Olsen, Charles

    D)_____

       Olsen, Christopher

    E)_____

3._____

4. <u>DeMattia, Jessica</u>

    A)_____

       DeLong, Jesse

    B)_____

       DeMatteo, Jessie

    C)_____

       Derby, Jessie S.

    D)_____

       DeShazo, L.M.

    E)_____

4._____

Question 5.

DIRECTIONS: Following are a group of four related sentences, which may or may not be in logical order. Following the sentences are five suggested sequences, lettered A, B, C, D, and E, from which you are to select the one that indicates the best arrangement of sentences. Indicate your choice of letters in the space at right.

5. (1) It must be comparatively scarce, and it should have a stable value.
   (2) In order to serve satisfactorily as money, a substance must have certain qualities.
   (3) It should also be durable, and its value should be high in proportion to its bulk.
   (4) Gold and silver have been widely used for money because they possess these qualities to a greater extent than do other commodities.

    A. 2-4-1-3
    B. 2-3-1-4
    C. 2-1-4-3
    D. 2-1-3-4
    E. 2-4-3-1

5._____

Question 6.

DIRECTIONS: Following is a sentence with an underlined word that is spelled as it is pronounced. Write the correct spelling of the word in the blank. Then decide which one of the suggested answers, A, B, C, or D, is the correct answer to the question, and write the letter in the space at right.

6. The new treasurer uses the same system that his pred-eh-sess´-urr did. In the correct spelling, _____, what is the tenth letter?
    A. s
    B. e
    C. o
    D. none of the above

6._____

Questions 7-11.

DIRECTIONS: In each line there are three names or numbers that are much alike.
Compare the three names or numbers and decide which ones are
exactly alike. Fill in the letter
A. if ALL THREE names or number are exactly ALIKE
B. if only the FIRST and SECOND names or numbers are exactly ALIKE
C. if only the FIRST and THIRD names or numbers are exactly ALIKE
D. if only the SECOND and THIRD names or numbers are exactly ALIKE
E. if ALL THREE names or numbers are DIFFERENT

7. Davis Hazen	David Hozen	David Hazen	7._____
8. Lois Appel	Lois Appel	Lois Apfel	8._____
9. June Allan	Jane Allan	Jane Allan	9._____
10. 10235	10235	10235	10._____
11. 32614	32164	32614	11._____

Questions 12-22.

DIRECTIONS: Compute the answer and compare it with suggested answers. Mark
the letter in the space at right.

12. Add: 12._____

963
257
+416

A. 1,516
B. 1,526
C. 1,636
D. 1,726
E. none of the above

64

5.(#2)

13. Add: 13._____

    22
    +33

        A. 44
        B. 45
        C. 54
        D. 55
        E. none of the above

14. Add: 14._____

    5.2 + .96 + 47.0 =

        A. 19.5
        B. 48.48
        C. 53.16
        D. 42.98
        E. none of the above

15. Subtract: 15._____

    24
    - 3

        A. 20
        B. 21
        C. 27
        D. 29
        E. none of the above

16. Subtract: 16._____

    33
    -8

        A. 25
        B. 26
        C. 35
        D. 36
        E. none of the above

17. Subtract:

    219
    -110

    A. 99
    B. 109
    C. 199
    D. 189
    E. none of the above

17._____

18. Multiply:

    25
    X5

    A. 100
    B. 115
    C. 125
    D. 135
    E. none of the above

18._____

19. Multiply:

    45
    X5

    A. 200
    B. 215
    C. 225
    D. 235
    E. none of the above

19._____

20. 47% of 538 =

    A. 11.45
    B. 252.86
    C. 285.14
    D. 265.66
    E. none of the above

20._____

21. Divide:

    6$\overline{)126}$

    A. 20
    B. 22
    C. 24
    D. 26
    E. none of the above

21._____

22. Divide:

22._____

$$40\overline{)1{,}208}$$

A. 3
B. 30
C. 33
D. 40
E. none of the above

Questions 23-32.

DIRECTIONS: For each question, find which one of the suggested answers contains numbers and letters all of which appear in that question. These numbers and letters may be in any order in the question, but all four must appear. If neither A, B, C, nor D fits, mark E for that question. Mark your answer in the space at right.

23. 8 N K 9 G T 4 6   23._____

24. T 9 7 Z 6 L 3 K   24._____

25. Z 7 G K 3 9 8 N   25._____

26. 3 K 9 4 6 G Z L   26._____

27. Z N 7 3 8 K T 9   27._____

Suggested Answers for Questions 23-27:
A = 7, 9, G, K
B = 8, 9, T, Z
C = 6, 7, K, Z
D = 6, 8, G, T
E = none of the above

28. 2 3 P 6 V Z 4 L   28._____

29. T 7 4 3 P Z 9 G   29._____

30. 6 N G Z 3 9 P 7   30._____

31. 9 6 P 4 N G Z 2   31._____

32. 4 9 7 T L P 3 V   32._____

Suggested Answers for Questions 28-32:
A = 3, 6, G, P
B = 3, 7, P, V
C = 4, 6, V, Z
D = 4, 7, G, Z
E = none of the above

Questions 33-34.

DIRECTIONS: Consider the figures below to be correct figures.

The figures below are incorrect because the slope of one of the lines differs from the slope in one of the similar correct figures.

The following questions show four correct figures and one incorrect figure. Select the letter of the incorrect figure and mark the letter in the space at right.

33.   A   B   C   D   E   33._____

9.(#2)

34.

| A | B | C | D | E |

34._____

Questions 35-48

DIRECTIONS: On the left is a series of numbers or letters which follow some definite order. Pick the answer that follows the order and write the letter of your choice in the space at right.

35. x c x d x e x

A. f x
B. f g
C. x f
D. e f
E. x g

35._____

36. a b d c e f h

A. c h
B. i g
C. g i
D. k l
E. i h

36._____

37. 15 14 13 12 11 10 9

A. 2 1
B. 17 16
C. 8 9
D. 8 7
E. 9 8

37._____

38. 20 20 21 21 22 22 23

A. 23 23
B. 23 24
C. 19 19
D. 22 23
E. 21 22

38._____

39. 17 3 17 4 17 5 17

    A. 6 17
    B. 6 7
    C. 17 6
    D. 5 6
    E. 17 7

40. 1 2 4 5 7 8 10

    A. 11 12
    B. 12 14
    C. 10 13
    D. 12 13
    E. 11 13

41. 21 21 20 20 19 19 18

    A. 18 18
    B. 18 17
    C. 17 18
    D. 17 17
    E. 18 19

42. 1 20 3 19 5 18 7

    A. 8 9
    B. 8 17
    C. 17 10
    D. 17 9
    E. 9 18

43. 30 2 28 4 26 6 24

    A. 23 9
    B. 26 8
    C. 8 9
    D. 26 22
    E. 8 22

44. 5 6 20 7 8 19 9

    A. 10 18
    B. 18 17
    C. 10 17
    D. 18 19
    E. 10 11

45. 9 10 1 11 12 2 13   45._____

    A. 2 14
    B. 3 14
    C. 14 3
    D. 14 15
    E. 14 1

46. 4 6 9 11 14 16 19   46._____

    A. 21 24
    B. 22 25
    C. 20 22
    D. 21 23
    E. 22 24

47. 8 8 1 10 10 3 12   47._____

    A. 13 13
    B. 12 5
    C. 12 4
    D. 13 5
    E. 4 12

48. 20 21 23 24 27 28 32 33 38 39   48._____

    A. 45 46
    B. 45 54
    C. 44 45
    D. 44 49
    E. 40 46

Questions 49-53.

DIRECTIONS: Each of the following questions consists of two sets of symbols.
Find the one rule that (a) explains the similarity of the symbols
within each set, and (b) also explains the difference between the
sets. Among the five suggested answers, find the symbol that can
best be substituted for the question mark in the second set. In all
these questions you will find details that have nothing to do with the
principle of the question: to find the similarity between the symbols
within a set and the difference between the sets. Mark the letter of
your answer choice in the space at right.

49.   SET 1   SET 2   49._____

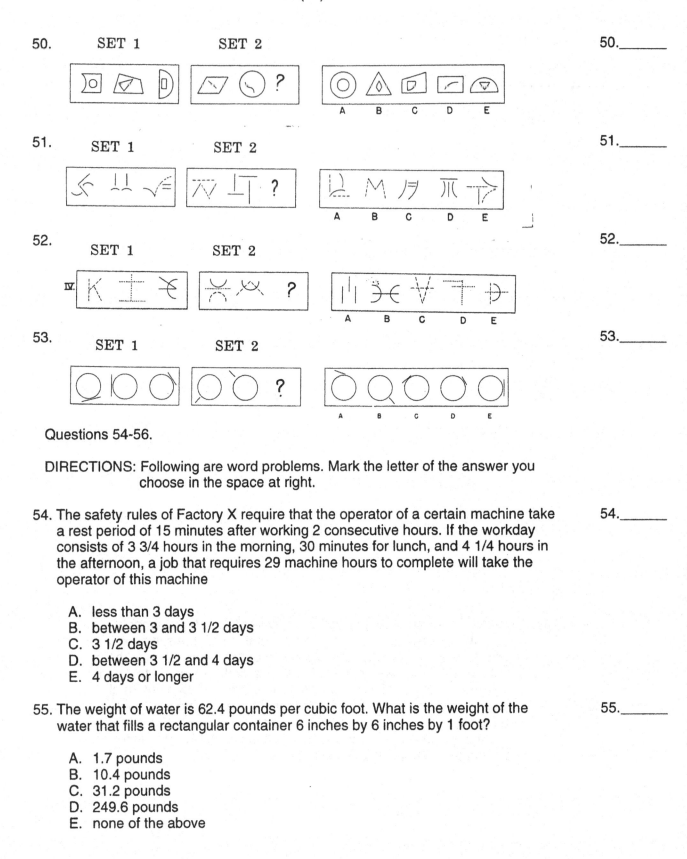

50. SET 1   SET 2   50._____

51. SET 1   SET 2   51._____

52. SET 1   SET 2   52._____

53. SET 1   SET 2   53._____

Questions 54-56.

DIRECTIONS: Following are word problems. Mark the letter of the answer you choose in the space at right.

54. The safety rules of Factory X require that the operator of a certain machine take a rest period of 15 minutes after working 2 consecutive hours. If the workday consists of 3 3/4 hours in the morning, 30 minutes for lunch, and 4 1/4 hours in the afternoon, a job that requires 29 machine hours to complete will take the operator of this machine   54._____

   A. less than 3 days
   B. between 3 and 3 1/2 days
   C. 3 1/2 days
   D. between 3 1/2 and 4 days
   E. 4 days or longer

55. The weight of water is 62.4 pounds per cubic foot. What is the weight of the water that fills a rectangular container 6 inches by 6 inches by 1 foot?   55._____

   A. 1.7 pounds
   B. 10.4 pounds
   C. 31.2 pounds
   D. 249.6 pounds
   E. none of the above

56. The inventor of a machine which operates by solar heat claims that it accumulates heat in the daytime at the rate of 10 units an hour on sunny days and 3 units an hour on cloudy days. During rain there is no accumulation of heat. In July there were 22 hours of daylight rain and 42 hours of cloudy daylight. Assuming on the average 13 hours of daylight per day in July, how many units should the machine have accumulated that month?

56._____

   A. 339
   B. 403
   C. 3,516
   D. 3,810
   E. none of the above

Questions 57-60

DIRECTIONS: Refer to the tables and charts to answer the following questions, and mark the letter of the correct answer in the space at right.

CONSUMPTION OF FUELS FOR PRODUCTION OF ELECTRIC ENERGY
1998-2003

	1998	1999	2000	2001	2002	2003
Bituminous and lignite coal (thousands short tons)	165,794	173,882	179,612	190,941	200,198	223,162
Anthracite coal (thousands short tons)	2,629	2,751	2,509	2,297	2,139	2,289
Fuel oil (thousands of barrels)	88,263	85,340	85,736	85,768	93,314	101,162
Gas (millions of cubic feet)	1,628,509	1,724,762	1,825,117	1,955,974	2,144,473	2,321,889

57. In which year did the greatest number of kinds of fuel show an increase in consumption over that of the preceding year?

57._____

   A. 1999
   B. 2000
   C. 2001
   D. 2002
   E. 2003

58. The total amount of coal consumed in the production of electric energy in 2003   58._____
    was approximately what percent of that consumed in 1998?

    A. 57%
    B. 75%
    C. 134%
    D. 150%
    E. 168%

POPULATION MOVEMENT TO AND FROM COUNTY X
1982 TO 2003

MOVING TO COUNTY ···········
MOVING FROM COUNTY ——————

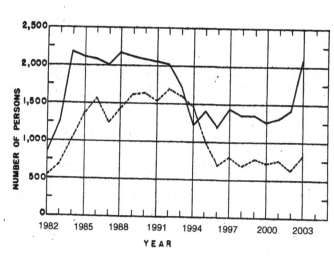

59. The graph above indicates that, with respect to County X, migratory activities   59._____
    during the period from 1982 to 2003 tended mostly to result in

    A. population gains
    B. population losses
    C. gradual stabilization of population
    D. irregular fluctuations in population without consistent direction
    E. cycles of alternating losses and gains in population which tended to
       balance each other

60. The ratio of the number of persons who left to the number who entered County X   60._____
    in 2003 is approximately

    A. 12 to 7
    B. 7 to 12
    C. 2 to 5
    D. 5 to 2
    E. 5 to 3

KEY (CORRECT ANSWERS)

1.	D	16.	A	31.	E	46.	A
2.	E	17.	B	32.	B	47.	B
3.	B	18.	C	33.	A	48.	A
4.	C	19.	C	34.	B	49.	E
5.	D	20.	B	35.	A	50.	D
6.	C	21.	E	36.	C	51.	B
7.	E	22.	E	37.	D	52.	E
8.	B	23.	D	38.	B	53.	B
9.	D	24.	C	39.	A	54.	D
10.	A	25.	A	40.	E	55.	E
11.	C	26.	E	41.	B	56.	C
12.	C	27.	B	42.	D	57.	E
13.	D	28.	C	43.	E	58.	C
14.	C	29.	D	44.	A	59.	B
15.	B	30.	A	45.	C	60.	D

EXAMINATION SECTION
TEST 1

DIRECTIONS: Each question or incomplete statement is followed by several suggested answers or completions. Select the one that *BEST* answers the question or completes the statement. *PRINT THE LETTER OF THE CORRECT ANSWER IN THE SPACE AT THE RIGHT.*

READING COMPREHENSION.

Questions 1-4. Read the passage below and answer the following questions by selecting the best of the five suggested answers.

Visitors will arrive at the north gate in six 17-passenger buses. An automobile from the installation will bring three visiting officials to this gate. The automobile will arrive at 2:00 p.m. Two of the buses will arrive there at 2:20 p.m. and the others at 2:40 p.m. The vehicles will move from the gate south along Hamilton Street to Main Avenue. They will proceed east on Main, and discharge the passengers at the foot of the steps at the front of the Headquarters Building. Four of the buses and the automobile will wait to load those visitors who are going to the southwest area. Two of the buses will rejoin the shuttle bus service for the installation.

1. The gate to which the visitors are to come is the   1._____

    A. north
    B. south
    C. east
    D. west
    E. southeast

2. The number of buses to be used to bring visitors to the gate specified is   2._____

    A. 2
    B. 6
    C. 7
    D. 10
    E. 17

3. The number of vehicles that will wait at the Headquarters Building to carry visitors and   3._____
    visiting officials to the southwest area is

    A. 1
    B. 2
    C. 4
    D. 5
    E. 6

4. The visiting officials will be riding in_____.   4._____

    A. the leading bus
    B. an automobile
    C. a bus arriving at 2:20 p.m.
    D. the last bus to arrive
    E. several buses

Question 5-6. Answer the question below based on the following passages.

What constitutes skill in any line of work is not always easy to determine; economy of time must be carefully distinguished from economy of energy, as the quickest method may require the greatest expenditure of muscular effort, and may not be essential or at all desirable.

5. *The passage best supports the statement that*   5.____

    A.   energy and time cannot both be conserved in the performing of a single task
    B.   the most efficiently executed task is not always the one done in the shortest time
    C.   if a task requires muscular energy, it is not being performed economically
    D.   skill in performing a task should not be acquired at the expense of time
    E.   a task is well done when it is performed in the shortest time

In the business districts of cities, collections from street letter boxes are made at stated hours, and collectors are required to observe these hours exactly. Any businessman using these boxes can rely with certainty upon the time of the next collection.

6. *The passage best supports the statement that* an important characteristic of mail collec-   6.____
tions is their

    A.   cheapness
    B.   extent
    C.   safety
    D.   speed
    E.   regularity

VERBAL ABILITIES.

Questions 7-8. For each question, choose the one of the five suggested answers that means the most nearly the same as the word in *italics.*

7. A small crane was used to *raise* the heavy parts.   7.____
Raise means most nearly

    A.   drag
    B.   unload
    C.   deliver
    D.   lift
    E.   guide

8. The reports were *consolidated* by the secretary. *Consolidated* means most nearly   8.____

    A.   combined
    B.   concluded
    C.   distributed
    D.   protected
    E.   weighed

Questions 9-11. For each question, select the word or group of words lettered A, B, C, D, or E that means most nearly the same as the word in capital letters.

9. PREVIOUS means most nearly   9._____

   A. abandoned
   B. former
   C. timely
   D. successive
   E. younger

10. To ENCOUNTER means most nearly to   10._____

   A. recall
   B. overcome
   C. weaken
   D. retreat
   E. meet

11. A FUNDAMENTAL point is one that is   11._____

   A. difficult
   B. drastic
   C. essential
   D. emphasized
   E. final

NUMBER AND NAME COMPARISONS

Questions 12-14. In each line across the page there are three names or numbers that are much alike. Compare the three names or numbers and decide which ones are exactly alike. Choose the letter:

A) if ALL THREE names or numbers are exactly ALIKE
B) if only the FIRST and SECOND names or numbers are exactly ALIKE
C) if only the FIRST and THIRD names or numbers are exactly ALIKE
D) if only the SECOND and THIRD names or numbers are exactly ALIKE
E) if ALL THREE names or numbers are DIFFERENT

12.   June Allan Jane Allan Jane Allan   12._____

13.   10235   10235   10235   13._____

14.   32614   32164   32614   14._____

Questions 15-52. Each of the boxes below is labeled A, B, C, D, or E and contains the names of several people. Each question following is a name. For each question, choose the letter A, B, C, D, or E, depending upon which of these boxes the name is in.

A	B	C	D	E
Redman	Denton	Teller	Edison	Wheeler
Payne	Rayburn	Moore	Miller	Forest
Carter	Sanford	Garvey	Appleton	Simmons
Conlow	Eastlake	Randall	Loman	Camp

15.	Loman	15.____
16.	Edison	16.____
17.	Eastlake	17.____
18.	Garvey	18.____
19.	Payne	19.____
20.	Miller	20.____
21.	Redman	21.____
22.	Carter	22.____
23.	Denton	23.____
24.	Sanford	24.____
25.	Denton	25.____
26.	Payne	26.____
27.	Simmons	27.____
28.	Edison	28.____
29.	Conlow	29.____
30.	Randall	30.____
31.	Conlow	31.____
32.	Rayburn	32.____
33.	Eastlake	33.____
34.	Appleton	34.____
35.	Teller	35.____
36.	Simmons	36.____
37.	Payne	37.____
38.	Camp	38.____
39.	Miller	39.____
40.	Garvey	40.____
41.	Randall	41.____
42.	Wheeler	42.____
43.	Redman	43.____

44. Moore   44._____

45. Appleton   45._____

46. Forest   46._____

47. Moore   47._____

48. Teller   48._____

49. Carter   49._____

50. Wheeler   50._____

51. Edison   51._____

52. Rayburn   52._____

Questions 53-70. You will be given addresses to compare. Choose the letter A if the two addresses are exactly *Alike* in every way. Choose the letter D if they are *Different*.

53.	2134 S 20th St	2134 S 20th St	53._____
54.	4608 N Warnock St	4806 N Warnock St	54._____
55.	1202 W Girard Dr	1202 WGirard Rd	55._____
56.	3120 S Harcourt St	3120 S Harcourt St	56._____
57.	4618 WAddison St	4618 E Addison St	57._____
58.	39-B Parkway Rd	39-D Parkway Rd	58._____
59.	6425 N Delancey	6425 N Delancey	59._____
60.	5407 Columbia Rd	5407 Columbia Rd	60._____
61.	2106 Southern Ave	2106 Southern Ave	61._____
62.	HightailsN C	Highlands N C	62._____
63.	2873 Pershing Dr	2873 Pershing Dr	63._____
64.	1329 N H Ave NW	1329 N J Ave NW	64._____
65.	1316 N Quinn St Arl	1316 N Quinn St Alex	65._____
66.	7507 Wyngate Dr	7505 Wyngate Dr	66._____
67.	2918 Colesville Rd	2918 Colesville Rd	67._____
68.	2071 Belvedere Dr	2071 Belvedere Dr	68._____
69.	Palmer Wash	Palmer Mich	69._____
70.	2106 16th St SW	2106 16th St SW	70._____

MATHEMATICAL ABILITY

Questions 71-75. Solve each problem and see which of the suggested answers A, B, C, or D is correct. If your answer does not exactly agree with any of the four suggested answers, choose letter E.

71. Add:

963
257
416

    71._____

  A. 1,516   B. 1,526   C. 1,636   D. 1,726
  E. none of these

72. Subtract:

33
 8
—

    72._____

  A. 25   B. 26   C. 35   D. 36
  E. none of these

73. Multiply:

45
 5
—

    73._____

  A. 200   B. 215   C. 225   D. 235
  E. none of these

74. Divide:

$40\sqrt{1,208}$

    74._____

  A. 3   B. 30   C. 33   D. 40
  E. none of these

75. If 2 men can distribute 7,000 letters in 2 hours, in how many hours would they distribute 17,500 letters, at the same rate?

    75._____

  A. 3 hours   B. 4 1/2 hours   C. 5 hours   D. 10 hours
  E. none of these

————

KEY (CORRECT ANSWERS)

1.	A	16.	D	31.	A	46.	E	61.	A
2.	B	17.	B	32.	B	47.	C	62.	D
3.	D	18.	C	33.	B	48.	C	63.	A
4.	B	19.	A	34.	D	49.	A	64.	D
5.	B	20.	D	35.	C	50.	E	65.	D
6.	E	21.	A	36.	E	51.	D	66.	D
7.	D	22.	A	37.	A	52.	B	67.	A
8.	A	23.	B	38.	E	53.	A	68.	A
9.	B	24.	B	39.	D	54.	D	69.	D
10.	E	25.	B	40.	C	55.	D	70.	A
11.	C	26.	A	41.	C	56.	A	71.	C
12.	D	27.	E	42.	E	57.	D	72.	A
13.	A	28.	D	43.	A	58.	D	73.	C
14.	C	29.	A	44.	C	59.	A	74.	E
15.	D	30.	C	45.	D	60.	A	75.	C

SPELLING

COMMENTARY

Spelling forms an integral part of tests of academic aptitude and achievement and of general and mental ability. Moreover, the spelling question is a staple of verbal and clerical tests in civil service entrance and promotional examinations.

Perhaps, the most rewarding way to learn to spell successfully is the direct, functional approach of learning to spell correctly, both orally and in writing, all words as they appear, both singly and in context.

In accordance with this positive method, the spelling question is presented here in "test" form, as it might appear on an actual examination.

The spelling question may appear on examinations in the following format:

Four words are listed in each question. These are lettered A, B, C, and D. A fifth option, E, is also given, which always reads "none misspelled." The examinee is to select one of the five (lettered) choices: either A, B, C, or D if one of the words is misspelled, or item E, none misspelled, if all four words have been correctly spelled in the question.

SAMPLE QUESTIONS

The directions for this part are approximately as follows:

DIRECTIONS: Mark the space corresponding to the one MISSPELLED word in each of the following groups of words. If NO word is misspelled, mark the last space on the answer sheet.

SAMPLE O
A. walk
B. talk
C. play
D. dance
E. *none misspelled*

Since none of the words is misspelled, E would be marked on the answer sheet.

SAMPLE OO
A. seize
B. yield
C. define
D. reccless
E. *none misspelled*

Since "reccless" (correct spelling, reckless) has been misspelled, D would be marked on the answer. sheet

CLERICAL ABILITIES TEST

EXAMINATION SECTION
TEST 1

DIRECTIONS: Each question or incomplete statement is followed by several suggested answers or completions. Select the one that *BEST* answers the question or completes the statement. *PRINT THE LETTER OF THE CORRECT ANSWER IN THE SPACE AT THE RIGHT.*

Questions 1-10.

DIRECTIONS: Questions 1 through 10 consist of lines of names, dates and numbers. For each question, you are to choose the option (A, B, C, or D) in Column II which *EXACTLY* matches the information in Column I. *PRINT THE LETTER OF THE CORRECT ANSWER IN THE SPACE AT THE RIGHT.*

SAMPLE QUESTION

Column I		Column II	
Schneider 11/16/75 581932	A. Schneider	11/16/75	518932
	B. Schneider	11/16/75	581932
	C. Schnieder	11/16/75	581932
	D. Shnieder	11/16/75	518932

The correct answer is B. Only option B shows the name, date and number exactly as they are in Column I. Option A has a mistake in the number. Option C has a mistake in the name. Option D has a mistake in the name and in the number. Now answer Questions 1 through 10 in the same manner.

Column I		Column II	
1. Johnston 12/26/74 659251	A. Johnson 12/23/74 659251		1._____
	B. Johston 12/26/74 659251		
	C. Johnston 12/26/74 695251		
	D. Johnston 12/26/74 659251		
2. Allison 1/26/75 9939256	A. Allison 1/26/75 9939256		2._____
	B. Alisson 1/26/75 9939256		
	C. Allison 1/26/76 9399256		
	D. Allison 1/26/75 9993256		
3. Farrell 2/12/75 361251	A. Farell 2/21/75 361251		3._____
	B. Farrell 2/12/75 361251		
	C. Farrell 2/21/75 361251		
	D. Farrell 2/12/75 361151		
4. Guerrero 4/28/72 105689	A. Guererro 4/28/72 105689		4._____
	B. Guererro 4/28/72 105986		
	C. Guerrero 4/28/72 105869		
	D. Guerrero 4/28/72 105689		

5. McDonnell 6/05/73 478215

    A. McDonnell 6/15/73 478215
    B. McDonnell 6/05/73 478215
    C. McDonnell 6/05/73 472815
    D. MacDonell 6/05/73 478215

    5.____

6. Shepard 3/31/71 075421

    A. Sheperd 3/31/71 075421
    B. Shepard 3/13/71 075421
    C. Shepard 3/31/71 075421
    D. Shepard 3/13/71 075241

    6.____

7. Russell 4/01/69 031429

    A. Russell 4/01/69 031429
    B. Russell 4/10/69 034129
    C. Russell 4/10/69 031429
    D. Russell 4/01/69 034129

    7.____

8. Phillips 10/16/68 961042

    A. Philipps 10/16/68 961042
    B. Phillips 10/16/68 960142
    C. Phillips 10/16/68 961042
    D. Philipps 10/16/68 916042

    8.____

9. Campbell 11/21/72 624856

    A. Campbell 11/21/72 624856
    B. Campbell 11/21/72 624586
    C. Campbell 11/21/72 624686
    D. Campbel 11/21/72 624856

    9.____

10. Patterson 9/18/71 76199176

    A. Patterson 9/18/72 76191976
    B. Patterson 9/18/71 76199176
    C. Patterson 9/18/72 76199176
    D. Patterson 9/18/71 76919176

    10.____

Questions 11-15.

DIRECTIONS: Questions 11 through 15 consist of groups of numbers and letters which you are to compare. For each question, you are to choose the option (A, B, C, or D) in Column II which *EXACTLY* matches the group of numbers and letters given in Column I.

SAMPLE QUESTION

Column I
B92466

Column II
A. B92644
B. B94266
C. A92466
D. B92466

The correct answer is D. Only option D in Column II shows the group of numbers and letters *EXACTLY* as it appears in Column I. Now answer Questions 11 through 15 in the same manner.

Column I
11.   925AC5

Column II
A. 952CA5
B. 925AC5
C. 952AC5
D. 925CA6

12.   Y006925

    A. Y060925
    B. Y006295
    C. Y006529
    D. Y006925

13.   J236956

    A. J236956
    B. J326965
    C. J239656
    D. J932656

14.   AB6952

    A. AB6952
    B. AB9625
    C. AB9652
    D. AB6925

15.   X259361

    A. X529361
    B. X259631
    C. X523961
    D. X259361

Questions 16-25.

DIRECTIONS: Each of Questions 16 through 25 consists of three lines of code letters and three lines of numbers. The numbers on each line should correspond with the code letters on the same line in accordance with the table below.

Code Letter	S	V	W	A	Q	M	X	E	G	K
Corresponding Number	0	1	2	3	4	5	6	7	8	9

On some of the lines, an error exists in the coding. Compare the letters and numbers in each question carefully. If you find an error or errors on:

only *one* of the lines in the question, mark your answer A;
any *two* lines in the question, mark your answer B;
all *three* lines in the question, mark your answer C;
none of the lines in the question, mark your answer D.

SAMPLE QUESTION

WQGKSXG   2489068
XEKVQMA   6591453
KMAESXV   9527061

In the above example, the first line is correct since each code letter listed has the correct corresponding number. On the second line, an error exists because code letter E should have the number 7 instead of the number 5. On the third line an error exists because the code letter A should have the number 3 instead of the number 2. Since there are errors in two of the three lines, the correct answer is B. Now answer Questions 16 through 25 in the same manner.

16.   SWQEKGA   0247983   16._____
      KEAVSXM   9731065
      SSAXGKQ   0036894

17.   QAMKMVS   4259510   17._____
      MGGEASX   5897306
      KSWMKWS   9125920

18.	WKXQWVE QKXXQVA AWMXGVS	2964217 4966413 3253810	18._____
19.	GMMKASE AWVSKSW QAVSVGK	8559307 3210902 4310189	19._____
20.	XGKQSMK QSVKEAS GSMXKMV	6894049 4019730 8057951	20._____
21.	AEKMWSG MKQSVQK XGQAEVW	3195208 5940149 6843712	21._____
22.	XGMKAVS SKMAWEQ GVMEQSA	6858310 0953174 8167403	22._____
23.	VQSKAVE WQGKAEM MEGKAWQ	1489317 2489375 5689324	23._____
24.	XMQVSKG QMEKEWS KMEVKGA	6541098 4579720 9571983	24._____
25.	GKVAMEW AXMVKAE KWAGMAV	8912572 3651937 9238531	25._____

Questions 26-35.

DIRECTIONS: Each of Questions 26 through 35 consists of a column of figures. For each question, add the column of figures and choose the correct answer from the four choices given.

26. 5,665.43
     2,356.69
     6,447.24
     <u>7,239.65</u>

    A. 20,698.01   B. 21,709.01
    C. 21,718.01   D. 22,609.01

26._____

27. 817,209.55
    264,354.29
     82,368.76
    <u>849,964.89</u>

    A. 1,893,997.49   B. 1,989,988.39
    C. 2,009,077.39   D. 2,013,897,49

27._____

28. 156,366.89
249,973.23
823,229.49
56,869.45

  A. 1,286,439.06   B. 1,287,521.06
  C. 1,297,539.06   D. 1,296,421.06

28.____

29. 23,422.15
149,696.24
238,377.53
86,289.79
505,544.63

  A. 989,229.34   B. 999,879.34
  C. 1,003,330.34   D. 1,023,329.34

29.____

30. 2,468,926.70
656,842.28
49,723.15
832,369.59

  A. 3,218,061.72   B. 3,808,092.72
  C. 4,007,861.72   D. 4,818,192.72

30.____

31. 524,201.52
7,775,678.51
8,345,299.63
40,628,898.08
31,374,670.07

  A. 88,646,647.81   B. 88,646,747.91
  C. 88,648,647.91   D. 88,648,747.81

31.____

32. 6,824,829.40
682,482.94
5,542,015.27
775,678.51
7,732,507.25

  A. 21,557,513.37   B. 21,567,513.37
  C. 22,567,503.37   D. 22,567,513.37

32.____

33. 22,109,405.58
6,097,093.43
5,050,073.99
8,118,050.05
4,313,980.82

  A. 45,688,593.87   B. 45,688,603.87
  C. 45,689,593.87   D. 45,689,603.87

33.____

34. 79,324,114.19
99,848,129.74
43,331,653.31
41,610,207.14

34.____

A. 264,114,104.38   B. 264,114,114.38
C. 265,114,114.38   D. 265,214,104.38

35.   33,729,653.94   35.____
        5,959,342.58
       26,052,715.47
        4,452,669.52
        7,079,953.59

A. 76,374,334.10   B. 76,375,334.10
C. 77,274,335.10   D. 77,275,335.10

Questions 36-40.

DIRECTIONS: Each of Questions 36 through 40 consists of a single number in Column I and
               four options in Column II. For each question, you are to choose the option (A,
               B, C, or D) in Column II which *EXACTLY* matches the number in Column I.
                              SAMPLE QUESTION
                Column I   Column II
                5965121   A.   5956121
                                             B.   5965121
                                             C.   5966121
                                             D.   5965211

The correct answer is B. Only option B shows the number *EXACTLY* as it appears in Column I.
Now answer Questions 36 through 40 in the same manner.

	Column I	Column II	
36.	9643242	A.	9643242
		B.	9462342
		C.	9642442
		D.	9463242
37.	3572477	A.	3752477
		B.	3725477
		C.	3572477
		D.	3574277
38.	5276101	A.	5267101
		B.	5726011
		C.	5271601
		D.	5276101
39.	4469329	A.	4496329
		B.	4469329
		C.	4496239
		D.	4469239
40.	2326308	A.	2236308
		B.	2233608
		C.	2326308
		D.	2323608

KEY (CORRECT ANSWERS)

1. D	11. B	21. A	31. D
2. A	12. D	22. C	32. A
3. B	13. A	23. B	33. B
4. D	14. A	24. D	34. A
5. B	15. D	25. A	35. C
6. C	16. D	26. B	36. A
7. A	17. C	27. D	37. C
8. C	18. A	28. A	38. D
9. A	19. D	29. C	39. B
10. B	20. B	30. C	40. C

TEST 2

Questions 1-5.

DIRECTIONS: Each of Questions 1 through 5 consists of a name and a dollar amount. In each question, the name and dollar amount in Column II should be an exact copy of the name and dollar amount in Column I. If there is:

a mistake only in the name, mark your answer A;
a mistake only in the dollar amount, mark your answer B;
a mistake in both the name and the dollar amount, mark your answer C;
no mistake in either the name or the dollar amount, mark your answer D.

SAMPLE QUESTION

Column I	Column II
George Peterson	George Petersson
$125.50	$125.50

Compare the name and dollar amount in Column II with the name and dollar amount in Column I. The name *Petersson* in Column II is spelled *Peterson* in Column I. The amount is the same in both columns. Since there is a mistake only in the name, the answer to the sample question is A.

Now answer Questions 1 through 5 in the same manner.

Column I	Column II	
1. Susanne Shultz $3440	Susanne Schultz $3440	1._____
2. Anibal P. Contrucci $2121.61	Anibel P. Contrucci $2112.61	2._____
3. Eugenio Mendoza $12.45	Eugenio Mendozza $12.45	3._____
4. Maurice Gluckstadt $4297	Maurice Gluckstadt $4297	4._____
5. John Pampellonne $4656.94	John Pammpellonne $4566.94	5._____

Questions 6-11.

DIRECTIONS: Each of Questions 6 through 11 consists of a set of names and addresses which you are to compare. In each question, the name and addresses in Column II should be an *EXACT* copy of the name and address in Column I. If there is:

a mistake only in the name, mark your answer A;
a mistake only in the address, mark your answer B;
a mistake in both the name and address, mark your answer C;
no mistake in either the name or address, mark your answer D.

SAMPLE QUESTION

Column I	Column II
Michael Filbert	Michael Filbert
456 Reade Street	645 Reade Street
New York, N.	New York, N . Y. 10013

Since there is a mistake only in the address (the street number should be 456 instead of 645), the answer to the sample question is B.

Now answer Questions 6 through 11 in the same manner.

	Column I	Column II	

6. Hilda Goettelmann
    55 Lenox Rd.
    Brooklyn, N. Y. 11226

    Hilda Goettelman
    55 Lenox Ave.
    Brooklyn, N. Y. 11226

    6._____

7. Arthur Sherman
    2522 Batchelder St.
    Brooklyn, N. Y. 11235

    Arthur Sharman
    2522 Batcheder St.
    Brooklyn, N. Y. 11253

    7._____

8. Ralph Barnett
    300 West 28 Street
    New York, New York 10001

    Ralph Barnett
    300 West 28 Street
    New York, New York 10001

    8._____

9. George Goodwin
    135 Palmer Avenue
    Staten Island, New York 10302

    George Godwin
    135 Palmer Avenue
    Staten Island, New York 10302

    9._____

10. Alonso Ramirez
    232 West 79 Street
    New York, N. Y. 10024

    Alonso Ramirez
    223 West 79 Street
    New York, N. Y. 10024

    10._____

11. Cynthia Graham
    149-35 83 Street
    Howard Beach, N. Y. 11414

    Cynthia Graham
    149-35 83 Street
    Howard Beach, N. Y. 11414

    11._____

Questions 12-20.

DIRECTIONS: Questions 12 through 20 are problems in subtraction. For each question do the subtraction and select your answer from the four choices given.

12. 232,921.85
     -179,587.68   12._____

    A. 52,433.17   B. 52,434.17
    C. 53,334.17   D. 53,343.17

13. 5,531,876.29
     -3,897,158.36   13._____

    A. 1,634,717.93   B. 1,644,718.93
    C. 1,734,717.93   D. 1,734,718.93

14. 1,482,658.22
     - 937,925.76   14._____

    A. 544,633.46   B. 544,732.46
    C. 545,632.46   D. 545,732.46

15. 937,828.17
     -259,673.88   15._____

    A. 678,154.29   B. 679,154.29
    C. 688,155.39   D. 699,155.39

16. 760,412.38
    -263,465.95

    A. 496,046.43   B. 496,946.43
    C. 496,956.43   D. 497,046.43

16.___

17. 3,203,902.26
    -2,933,087.96

    A. 260,814.30   B. 269,824.30
    C. 270,814.30   D. 270,824.30

17.___

18. 1,023,468.71
    - 934,678.88

    A. 88,780.83   B. 88,789.83
    C. 88,880.83   D. 88,889.83

18.___

19. 831,549.47
    -772,814.78

    A. 58,734.69   B. 58,834.69
    C. 59,735,69   D. 59,834.69

19.___

20. 6,306,281.74
    -3,617,376.75

    A. 2,687,904.99   B. 2,688,904.99
    C. 2,689,804.99   D. 2,799,905.99

20.___

Questions 21-30.

DIRECTIONS: Each of Questions 21 through 30 consists of three lines of code letters and three lines of numbers. The numbers on each line should correspond with the code letters on the same line in accordance with the table below.

Code Letter	J	U	B	T	Y	D	K	R	L	P
Corresponding Number	0	1	2	3	4	5	6	7	8	9

On some of the lines, an error exists in the coding. Compare the letters and numbers in each question carefully. If you find an error or errors on:
    only *one* of the lines in the question, mark your answer A;
    any *two* lines in the question, mark your answer B;
    all *three* lines in the question, mark your answer C;
    none of the lines in the question, mark your answer D.

SAMPLE QUESTION

BJRPYUR   2079417
DTBPYKJ   5328460
YKLDBLT   4685283

In the above sample the first line is correct since each code letter listed has the correct corresponding number. On the second line, an error exists because code letter P should have the number 9 instead of the number 8. The third line is correct since each code letter listed has the correct corresponding number. Since there is an error in *one* of the three lines, the correct answer is A.

Now answer Questions 21 through 30 in the same manner.

21.	BYPDTJL	2495308	21.____
	PLRDTJU	9815301	
	DTJRYLK	5207486	
22.	RPBYRJK	7934706	22.____
	PKTYLBU	9624821	
	KDLPJYR	6489047	
23.	TPYBUJR	3942107	23.____
	BYRKPTU	2476931	
	DUKPYDL	5169458	
24.	KBYDLPL	6345898	24.____
	BLRKBRU	2876261	
	JTULDYB	0318542	
25.	LDPYDKR	8594567	25.____
	BDKDRJL	2565708	
	BDRPLUJ	2679810	
26.	PLRLBPU	9858291	26.____
	LPYKRDJ	8936750	
	TDKPDTR	3569527	
27.	RKURPBY	7617924	27.____
	RYUKPTJ	7426930	
	RTKPTJD	7369305	
28.	DYKPBJT	5469203	28.____
	KLPJBTL	6890238	
	TKPLBJP	3698209	
29.	BTPRJYL	2397148	29.____
	LDKUTYR	8561347	
	YDBLRPJ	4528190	
30.	ULPBKYT	1892643	30.____
	KPDTRBJ	6953720	
	YLKJPTB	4860932	

KEY (CORRECT ANSWERS)

1.	A		16.	B
2.	C		17.	C
3.	A		18.	B
4.	D		19.	A
5.	C		20.	B
6.	C		21.	B
7.	C		22.	C
8.	D		23.	D
9.	A		24.	B
10.	B		25.	A
11.	D		26.	C
12.	C		27.	A
13.	A		28.	D
14.	B		29.	B
15.	A		30.	D

CLERICAL ABILITIES

EXAMINATION SECTION
TEST 1

DIRECTIONS: Each question or incomplete statement is followed by several suggested answers or completions. Select the one that BEST answers the question or completes the statement. *PRINT THE LETTER OF THE CORRECT ANSWER IN THE SPACE AT THE RIGHT.*

Questions 1-4.

DIRECTIONS: Questions 1 through 4 are to be answered on the basis of the information given below.

The most commonly used filing system and the one that is easiest to learn is alphabetical filing. This involves putting records in an A to Z order, according to the letters of the alphabet. The name of a person is filed by using the following order: first, the surname or last name; second, the first name; third, the middle name or middle initial. For example, *Henry C. Young* is filed under *Y* and thereafter under *Young, Henry C.* The name of a company is filed in the same way. For example, *Long Cabinet Co.* is filed under *L,* while *John T. Long Cabinet Co.* is filed under *L* and thereafter under *Long., John T. Cabinet Co.*

1. The one of the following which lists the names of persons in the CORRECT alphabetical order is: 1.____

    A. Mary Carrie, Helen Carrol, James Carson, John Carter
    B. James Carson, Mary Carrie, John Carter, Helen Carrol
    C. Helen Carrol, James Carson, John Carter, Mary Carrie
    D. John Carter, Helen Carrol, Mary Carrie, James Carson

2. The one of the following which lists the names of persons in the CORRECT alphabetical order is: 2.____

    A. Jones, John C.; Jones, John A.; Jones, John P.; Jones, John K.
    B. Jones, John P.; Jones, John K.; Jones, John C.; Jones, John A.
    C. Jones, John A.; Jones, John C.; Jones, John K.; Jones, John P.
    D. Jones, John K.; Jones, John C.; Jones, John A.; Jones, John P.

3. The one of the following which lists the names of the companies in the CORRECT alpha-   3.____
betical order is:

    A. Blane Co., Blake Co., Block Co., Blear Co.
    B. Blake Co., Blane Co., Blear Co., Block Co.
    C. Block Co., Blear Co., Blane Co., Blake Co.
    D. Blear Co., Blake Co., Blane Co., Block Co.

4. You are to return to the file an index card on *Barry C. Wayne Materials and Supplies Co.*   4.____
Of the following, the CORRECT alphabetical group that you should return the index card to is

    A. A to G   B. H to M   C. N to S   D. T to Z

Questions 5-10.

DIRECTIONS: In each of Questions 5 through 10, the names of four people are given. For
each question, choose as your answer the one of the four names given which
should be filed FIRST according to the usual system of alphabetical filing of
names, as described in the following paragraph.

In filing names, you must start with the last name. Names are filed in order of the first letter of the last name, then the second letter, etc. Therefore, BAILY would be filed before
BROWN, which would be filed before COLT. A name with fewer letters of the same type
comes first; i.e., Smith before Smithe. If the last names are the same, the names are filed
alphabetically by the first name. If the first name is an initial, a name with an initial would
come before a first name that starts with the same letter as the initial. Therefore, I. BROWN
would come before IRA BROWN. Finally, if both last name and first name are the same, the
name would be filed alphabetically by the middle name, once again an initial coming before a
middle name which starts with the same letter as the initial. If there is no middle name at all,
the name would come before those with middle initials or names.

Sample Question: A.   Lester Daniels
                   B.   William Dancer
                   C.   Nathan Danzig
                   D.   Dan Lester

The last names beginning with D are filed before the last name beginning with L. Since
DANIELS, DANCER, and DANZIG all begin with the same three letters, you must look at the
fourth letter of the last name to determine which name should be filed first. C comes before I
or Z in the alphabet, so DANCER is filed before DANIELS or DANZIG. Therefore, the answer
to the above sample question is B.

5.   A.   Scott Biala   5.____
     B.   Mary Byala
     C.   Martin Baylor
     D.   Francis Bauer

6.   A.   Howard J. Black   6.____
     B.   Howard Black
     C.   J. Howard Black
     D.   John H. Black

7.   A.   Theodora Garth Kingston   7.____
     B.   Theadore Barth Kingston
     C.   Thomas Kingston
     D.   Thomas T. Kingston

8.   A.   Paulette Mary Huerta   8.____
     B.   Paul M. Huerta
     C.   Paulette L. Huerta
     D.   Peter A. Huerta

9. A. Martha Hunt Morgan
    B. Martin Hunt Morgan
    C. Mary H. Morgan
    D. Martine H. Morgan   9._____

10. A. James T. Meerschaum
    B. James M. Mershum
    C. James F. Mearshaum
    D. James N. Meshum   10._____

Questions 11-14.

DIRECTIONS: Questions 11 through 14 are to be answered SOLELY on the basis of the fol-
              lowing information.

    You are required to file various documents in file drawers which are labeled according to
the following pattern:

DOCUMENTS

MEMOS		LETTERS	
File	Subject	File	Subject
84PM1 - (A-L)		84PC1 - (A-L)	
84PM2 - (M-Z)		84PC2 - (M-Z)	

REPORTS		INQUIRIES	
File	Subject	File	Subject
84PR1 - (A-L)		84PQ1 - (A-L)	
84PR2 - (M-Z)		84PQ2 - (M-Z)	

11. A letter dealing with a burglary should be filed in the drawer labeled   11._____

    A. 84PM1   B. 84PC1   C. 84PR1   D. 84PQ2

12. A report on Statistics should be found in the drawer labeled   12._____

    A. 84PM1   B. 84PC2   C. 84PR2   D. 84PQ2

13. An inquiry is received about parade permit procedures. It should be filed in the drawer   13._____
    labeled

    A. 84PM2   B. 84PC1   C. 84PR1   D. 84PQ2

14. A police officer has a question about a robbery report you filed.   14._____
    You should pull this file from the drawer labeled

    A. 84PM1   B. 84PM2   C. 84PR1   D. 84PR2

Questions 15-22.

DIRECTIONS: Each of Questions 15 through 22 consists of four or six numbered names. For
              each question, choose the option (A, B, C, or D) which indicates the order in
              which the names should be filed in accordance with the following filing instruc-
              tions:
              - File alphabetically according to last name, then first name, then middle initial.
              - File according to each successive letter within a name.

- When comparing two names in which, the letters in the longer name are identical to the corresponding letters in the shorter name, the shorter name is filed first.
- When the last names are the same, initials are always filed before names beginning with the same letter.

15.
  I. Ralph Robinson
  II. Alfred Ross
  III. Luis Robles
  IV. James Roberts

The CORRECT filing sequence for the above names should be

A. IV, II, I, III
C. III, IV, I, II
B. I, IV, III, II
D. IV, I, III, II

15.___

16.
  I. Irwin Goodwin
  II. Inez Gonzalez
  III. Irene Goodman
  IV. Ira S. Goodwin
  V. Ruth I. Goldstein
  VI. M.B. Goodman

The CORRECT filing sequence for the above names should be

A. V, II, I, IV, III, VI
C. V, II, III, VI, IV, I
B. V, II, VI, III, IV, I
D. V, II, III, VI, I, IV

16.___

17.
  I. George Allan
  II. Gregory Allen
  III. Gary Allen
  IV. George Allen

The CORRECT filing sequence for the above names should be

A. IV, III, I, II
C. III, IV, I, II
B. I, IV, II, III
D. I, III, IV, II

17.___

18.
  I. Simon Kauffman
  II. Leo Kaufman
  III. Robert Kaufmann
  IV. Paul Kauffmann

The CORRECT filing sequence for the above names should be

A. I, IV, II, III
C. III, II, IV, I
B. II, IV, III, I
D. I, II, III, IV

18.___

19.
  I. Roberta Williams
  II. Robin Wilson
  III. Roberta Wilson
  IV. Robin Williams

The CORRECT filing sequence for the above names should be

A. III, II, IV, I
C. I, II, III, IV
B. I, IV, III, II
D. III, I, II, IV

19.___

20.
    I.   Lawrence Shultz
    II. Albert Schultz
    III. Theodore Schwartz
    IV. Thomas Schwarz
    V. Alvin Schultz
    VI. Leonard Shultz

The CORRECT filing sequence for the above names should be

20._____

  A. II, V, III, IV, I, VI
  C. II, V, I, VI, III, IV
  B. IV, III, V, I, II, VI
  D. I, VI, II, V, III, IV

21.
    I.   McArdle
    II. Mayer
    III. Maletz
    IV. McNiff
    V. Meyer
    VI. MacMahon

The CORRECT filing sequence for the above names should be

21._____

  A. I, IV, VI, III, II, V
  C. VI, III, II, I, IV, V
  B. II, I, IV, VI, III, V
  D. VI, III, II, V, I, IV

22.
    I.   Jack E. Johnson
    II. R.H. Jackson
    III. Bertha Jackson
    IV. J.T. Johnson
    V. Ann Johns
    VI. John Jacobs

The CORRECT filing sequence for the above names should be

22._____

  A. II, III, VI, V, IV, I
  C. VI, II, III, I, V, IV
  B. III, II, VI, V, IV, I
  D. III, II, VI, IV, V, I

Questions 23-30.

DIRECTIONS: The code table below shows 10 letters with matching numbers. For each question, there are three sets of letters. Each set of letters is followed by a set of numbers which may or may not match their correct letter according to the code table. For each question, check all three sets of letters and numbers and mark your answer:
    A. if no pairs are correctly matched
    B. if only one pair is correctly matched
    C. if only two pairs are correctly matched
    D. if all three pairs are correctly matched

CODE TABLE

T	M	V	D	S	P	R	G	B	H
1	2	3	4	5	6	7	8	9	0

<u>Sample Question:</u>   TMVDSP - 123456
                          RGBHTM - 789011
                          DSPRGB - 256789

In the sample question above, the first set of numbers correctly matches its set of letters. But the second and third pairs contain mistakes. In the second pair, M is incorrectly matched with number 1. According to the code table, letter M should be correctly matched with number 2. In the third pair, the letter D is incorrectly matched with number 2. According to the code table, letter D should be correctly matched with number 4. Since only one of the pairs is correctly matched, the answer to this sample question is B.

23. RSBMRM 759262
    GDSRVH 845730
    VDBRTM 349713

23._____

24. TGVSDR 183247
    SMHRDP 520647
    TRMHSR 172057

24._____

25. DSPRGM 456782
    MVDBHT 234902
    HPMDBT 062491

25._____

26. BVPTRD 936184
    GDPHMB 807029
    GMRHMV 827032

26._____

27. MGVRSH 283750
    TRDMBS 174295
    SPRMGV 567283

27._____

28. SGBSDM 489542
    MGHPTM 290612
    MPBMHT 269301

28._____

29. TDPBHM 146902
    VPBMRS 369275
    GDMBHM 842902

29._____

30. MVPTBV 236194
    PDRTMB 647128
    BGTMSM 981232

30._____

KEY (CORRECT ANSWERS)

1.	A	11.	B	21.	C
2.	C	12.	C	22.	B
3.	B	13.	D	23.	B
4.	D	14.	D	24.	B
5.	D	15.	D	25.	C
6.	B	16.	C	26.	A
7.	B	17.	D	27.	D
8.	B	18.	A	28.	A
9.	A	19.	B	29.	D
10.	C	20.	A	30.	A

———

TEST 2

Questions 1-10.

DIRECTIONS: Questions 1 through 10 each consists of two columns, each containing four lines of names, numbers and/or addresses. For each question, compare the lines in Column I with the lines in Column II to see if they match exactly, and mark your answer A, B, C, or D, according to the following instructions:

    A. all four lines match exactly
    B. only three lines match exactly
    C. only two lines match exactly
    D. only one line matches exactly

		COLUMN I	COLUMN II	
1.	I.	Earl Hodgson	Earl Hodgson	1._____
	II.	1409870	1408970	
	III.	Shore Ave.	Schore Ave.	
	IV.	Macon Rd.	Macon Rd.	
2.	I.	9671485	9671485	2._____
	II.	470 Astor Court	470 Astor Court	
	III.	Halprin, Phillip	Halperin, Phillip	
	IV.	Frank D. Poliseo	Frank D. Poliseo	
3.	I.	Tandem Associates	Tandom Associates	3._____
	II.	144-17 Northern Blvd.	144-17 Northern Blvd.	
	III.	Alberta Forchi	Albert Forchi	
	IV.	Kings Park, NY 10751	Kings Point, NY 10751	
4.	I.	Bertha C. McCormack	Bertha C. McCormack	4._____
	II.	Clayton, MO.	Clayton, MO.	
	III.	976-4242	976-4242	
	IV.	New City, NY 10951	New City, NY 10951	
5.	I.	George C. Morill	George C. Morrill	5._____
	II.	Columbia, SC 29201	Columbia, SD 29201	
	III.	Louis Ingham	Louis Ingham	
	IV.	3406 Forest Ave.	3406 Forest Ave.	
6.	I.	506 S. Elliott Pl.	506 S. Elliott Pl.	6._____
	II.	Herbert Hall	Hurbert Hall	
	III.	4712 Rockaway Pkway	4712 Rockaway Pkway	
	IV.	169 E. 7 St.	169 E. 7 St.	

	COLUMN I	COLUMN II	

7.
   I.   345 Park Ave.   345 Park Pl.   7.____
   II. Colman Oven Corp.   Coleman Oven Corp.
   III. Robert Conte   Robert Conti
   IV. 6179846   6179846

8.
   I.   Grigori Schierber   Grigori Schierber   8.____
   II. Des Moines, Iowa   Des Moines, Iowa
   III. Gouverneur Hospital Gouverneur Hospital
   IV. 91-35 Cresskill Pl. 91-35 Cresskill Pl.

9.
   I.   Jeffery Janssen   Jeffrey Janssen   9.____
   II. 8041071   8041071
   III. 40 Rockefeller Plaza 40 Rockafeller Plaza
   IV. 407 6 St.   406 7 St.

10.
   I.   5971996   5871996   10.____
   II. 3113 Knickerbocker Ave. 3113 Knickerbocker Ave.
   III. 8434 Boston Post Rd. 8424 Boston Post Rd.
   IV. Penn Station   Penn Station

Questions 11-14.

DIRECTIONS: Questions 11 through 14 are to be answered by looking at the four groups of names and addresses listed below (I, II, III, and IV) and then finding out the number of groups that have their corresponding numbered lines exactly the same.

GROUP I
Line 1. Richmond General Hospital
Line 2. Geriatric Clinic
Line 3. 3975 Paerdegat St.
Line 4 Loudonville, New York 11538

GROUP II
Richman General Hospital
Geriatric Clinic
3975 Peardegat St.
Londonville, New York 11538

GROUP III
Line 1. Richmond General Hospital
Line 2. Geriatric Clinic
Line 3. 3795 Paerdegat St.
Line 4. Loudonville, New York 11358

GROUP IV
Richmend General Hospital
Geriatric Clinic
3975 Paerdegat St.
Loudonville, New York 11538

11. In how many groups is line one exactly the same?   11.____

    A. Two   B. Three   C. Four   D. None

12. In how many groups is line two exactly the same?   12.____

    A. Two   B. Three   C. Four   D. None

13. In how many groups is line three exactly the same?   13.____

    A. Two   B. Three   C. Four   D. None

14. In how many groups is line four exactly the same?   14._____

    A. Two   B. Three   C. Four   D. None

Questions 15-18.

DIRECTIONS: Each of Questions 15 through 18 has two lists of names and addresses. Each list contains three sets of names and addresses. Check each of the three sets in the list on the right to see if they are the same as the corresponding set in the list on the left. Mark your answers:

    A. if none of the sets in the right list are the same as those in the left list
    B. if only one of the sets in the right list is the same as those in the left list
    C. if only two of the sets in the right list are the same as those in the left list
    D. if all three sets in the right list are the same as those in the left list

15.   Mary T. Berlinger   Mary T. Berlinger   15._____
        2351 Hampton St.   2351 Hampton St.
        Monsey, N.Y. 20117   Monsey, N.Y. 20117

        Eduardo Benes   Eduardo Benes
        473 Kingston Avenue   473 Kingston Avenue
        Central Islip, N.Y. 11734   Central Islip, N.Y. 11734

        Alan Carrington Fuchs   Alan Carrington Fuchs
        17 Gnarled Hollow Road   17 Gnarled Hollow Road
        Los Angeles, CA 91635   Los Angeles, CA 91685

16.   David John Jacobson   David John Jacobson   16._____
        178 35 St. Apt. 4C   178 53 St. Apt. 4C
        New York, N.Y. 00927   New York, N.Y. 00927

        Ann-Marie Calonella   Ann-Marie Calonella
        7243 South Ridge Blvd.   7243 South Ridge Blvd.
        Bakersfield, CA 96714   Bakersfield, CA 96714

        Pauline M. Thompson   Pauline M. Thomson
        872 Linden Ave.   872 Linden Ave.
        Houston, Texas 70321   Houston, Texas 70321

17.   Chester LeRoy Masterton   Chester LeRoy Masterson   17._____
        152 Lacy Rd.   152 Lacy Rd.
        Kankakee, Ill. 54532   Kankakee, Ill. 54532

        William Maloney   William Maloney
        S. LaCrosse Pla.   S. LaCross Pla.
        Wausau, Wisconsin 52146   Wausau, Wisconsin 52146

        Cynthia V. Barnes   Cynthia V. Barnes
        16 Pines Rd.   16 Pines Rd.
        Greenpoint, Miss. 20376   Greenpoint, Miss. 20376

18.   Marcel Jean Frontenac   Marcel Jean Frontenac   18.____
        8 Burton On The Water   6 Burton On The Water
        Calender, Me. 01471   Calender, Me. 01471

        J. Scott Marsden   J. Scott Marsden
        174 S. Tipton St.   174 Tipton St.
        Cleveland, Ohio   Cleveland, Ohio

        Lawrence T. Haney   Lawrence T. Haney
        171 McDonough St.   171 McDonough St.
        Decatur, Ga. 31304   Decatur, Ga. 31304

Questions 19-26.

DIRECTIONS: Each of Questions 19 through 26 has two lists of numbers. Each list contains three sets of numbers. Check each of the three sets in the list on the right to see if they are the same as the corresponding set in the list on the left. Mark your answers:
      A. if none of the sets in the right list are the same as those in the left list
      B. if only one of the sets in the right list is the same as those in the left list
      C. if only two of the sets in the right list are the same as those in the left list
      D. if all three sets in the right list are the same as those in the left list

19.   7354183476   7354983476   19.____
      4474747744   4474747774
      57914302311   57914302311

20.   7143592185   7143892185   20.____
      8344517699   8344518699
      9178531263   9178531263

21.   2572114731   257214731   21.____
      8806835476   8806835476
      8255831246   8255831246

22.   331476853821   331476858621   22.____
      6976658532996   6976655832996
      3766042113715   3766042113745

23.   8806663315   8806663315   23.____
      74477138449   74477138449
      211756663666   211756663666

24.   990006966996   99000696996   24.____
      53022219743   53022219843
      4171171117717   4171171177717

25.   24400222433004   24400222433004   25.____
      5300030055000355   5300030055500355
      20000075532002022   20000075532002022

26. 6111666406600001116   61116664066001116   26._____
    7111300117001100733   7111300117001100733
    26666446664476518   26666446664476518

Questions 27-30.

DIRECTIONS: Questions 27 through 30 are to be answered by picking the answer which is in the correct numerical order, from the lowest number to the highest number, in each question.

27. A. 44533, 44518, 44516, 44547   27._____
    B. 44516, 44518, 44533, 44547
    C. 44547, 44533, 44518, 44516
    D. 44518, 44516, 44547, 44533

28. A. 95587, 95593, 95601, 95620   28._____
    B. 95601, 95620, 95587, 95593
    C. 95593, 95587, 95601, 95620
    D. 95620, 95601, 95593, 95587

29. A. 232212, 232208, 232232, 232223   29._____
    B. 232208, 232223, 232212, 232232
    C. 232208, 232212, 232223, 232232
    D. 232223, 232232, 232208, 232212

30. A. 113419, 113521, 113462, 113588   30._____
    B. 113588, 113462, 113521, 113419
    C. 113521, 113588, 113419, 113462
    D. 113419, 113462, 113521, 113588

KEY (CORRECT ANSWERS)

1.	C	11.	A	21.	C
2.	B	12.	C	22.	A
3.	D	13.	A	23.	D
4.	A	14.	A	24.	A
5.	C	15.	C	25.	C
6.	B	16.	B	26.	C
7.	D	17.	B	27.	B
8.	A	18.	B	28.	A
9.	D	19.	B	29.	C
10.	C	20.	B	30.	D

RECORD KEEPING
EXAMINATION SECTION
TEST 1

DIRECTIONS: Each question or incomplete statement is followed by several suggested answers or completions. Select the one that BEST answers the question or completes the statement. *PRINT THE LETTER OF THE CORRECT ANSWER IN THE SPACE AT THE RIGHT.*

Questions 1-7.

DIRECTIONS: In answering Questions 1 through 7, use the following master list. For each question, determine where the name would fit on the master list. Each answer choice indicates right before or after the name in the answer choice.

Aaron, Jane
Armstead, Brendan
Bailey, Charles
Dent, Ricardo
Grant, Mark
Mars, Justin
Methieu, Justine
Parker, Cathy
Sampson, Suzy
Thomas, Heather

1. Schmidt, William   1._____
    A. Right before Cathy Parker   B. Right after Heather Thomas
    C. Right after Suzy Sampson   D. Right before Ricardo Dent

2. Asanti, Kendall   2._____
    A. Right before Jane Aaron   B. Right after Charles Bailey
    C. Right before Justine Methieu   D. Right after Brendan Armstead

3. O'Brien, Daniel   3._____
    A. Right after Justine Methieu   B. Right before Jane Aaron
    C. Right after Mark Grant   D. Right before Suzy Sampson

4. Marrow, Alison   4._____
    A. Right before Cathy Parker   B. Right before Justin Mars
    C. Right after Mark Grant   D. Right after Heather Thomas

5. Grantt, Marissa   5._____
    A. Right before Mark Grant   B. Right after Mark Grant
    C. Right after Justin Mars   D. Right before Suzy Sampson

6. Thompson, Heath   6.____
    A. Right after Justin Mars   B. Right before Suzy Sampson
    C. Right after Heather Thomas   D. Right before Cathy Parker

DIRECTIONS: Before answering Question 7, add in all of the names from Questions 1 through
              6. Then fit the name in alphabetical order based on the new list.

7. Francisco, Mildred   7.____
    A. Right before Mark Grant   B. Right after Marissa Grantt
    C. Right before Alison Marrow   D. Right after Kendall Asanti

Questions 8-10.

DIRECTIONS: In answering Questions 8 through 10, compare each pair of names and
              addresses. Indicate whether they are the same or different in any way.

8. William H. Pratt, J.D.   William H. Pratt, J.D.   8.____
    Attourney at Law   Attorney at Law
    A. No differences   B. 1 difference
    C. 2 differences   D. 3 differences

9. 1303 Theater Drive,; Apt. 3-B   1330 Theatre Drive,; Apt. 3-B   9.____
    A. No differences   B. 1 difference
    C. 2 differences   D. 3 differences

10. Petersdorff, Briana and Mary   Petersdorff, Briana and Mary   10.____
    A. No differences   B. 1 difference
    C. 2 differences   D. 3 differences

11. Which of the following words, if any, are misspelled?   11.____
    A. Affordable   B. Circumstansial
    C. Legalese   D. None of the above

Questions 12-13.

DIRECTIONS: Questions 12 and 13 are to be answered on the basis of the following table.

Standardized Test Results for High School Students in District #1230

	English	Math	Science	Reading
High School 1	21	22	15	18
High School 2	12	16	13	15
High School 3	16	18	21	17
High School 4	19	14	15	16

     The scores for each high school in the district were averaged out and listed for each
subject tested. Scores of 0-10 are significantly below College Readiness Standards. 11-15 are
below College Readiness, 16-20 meet College Readiness, and 21-25 are above College
Readiness.

12. If the high schools need to meet or exceed in at least half the categories   12.____
in order to NOT be considered "at risk," which schools are considered "at risk"?
    A. High School 2   B. High School 3
    C. High School 4   D. Both A and C

13. What percentage of subjects did the district as a whole meet or exceed   13.____
College Readiness standards?
    A. 25%   B. 50%   C. 75%   D. 100%

Questions 14-15.

DIRECTIONS: Questions 14 and 15 are to be answered on the basis of the following
information.

You have seven employees working as a part of your team: Austin, Emily, Jeremy,
Christina, Martin, Harriet, and Steve. You have just sent an e-mail informing them that
there will be a mandatory training session next week. To ensure that work still gets done,
you are offering the training twice during the week: once on Tuesday and also on
Thursday. This way half the employees will still be working while the other half attend the
training. The only other issue is that Jeremy doesn't work on Tuesdays and Harriet
doesn't work on Thursdays due to compressed work schedules.

14. Which of the following is a possible attendance roster for the first training   14.____
session?
    A. Emily, Jeremy, Steve   B. Steve, Christina, Harriet
    C. Harriet, Jeremy, Austin   D. Steve, Martin, Jeremy

15. If Harriet, Christina, and Steve attend the training session on Tuesday, which   15.____
of the following is a possible roster for Thursday's training session?
    A. Jeremy, Emily, and Austin   B. Emily, Martin, and Harriet
    C. Austin, Christina, and Emily   D. Jeremy, Emily, and Steve

Questions 16-20.

DIRECTIONS: In answering Questions 16 through 20, you will be given a word and will need
to choose the answer choice that is MOST similar or different to the word.

16. Which word means the SAME as *annual*?   16.____
    A. Monthly   B. Usually   C. Yearly   D. Constantly

17. Which word means the SAME as *effort*?   17.____
    A. Energy   B. Equate   C. Cherish   D. Commence

18. Which word means the OPPOSITE of *forlorn*?   18.____
    A. Neglected   B. Lethargy   C. Optimistic   D. Astonished

19. Which word means the SAME as *risk*?   19.____
    A. Admire   B. Hazard   C. Limit   D. Hesitant

20. Which word means the OPPOSITE of *translucent*?
    A. Opaque   B. Transparent   C. Luminous   D. Introverted

                                                                          20._____

21. Last year, Jamie's annual salary was $50,000. Her boss called her today to inform her that she would receive a 20% raise for the upcoming year. How much more money will Jamie receive next year?
    A. $60,000   B. $10,000   C. $1,000   D. $51,000

21._____

22. You and a co-worker work for a temp hiring agency as part of their office staff. You both are given 6 days off per month. How many days off are you and your co-worker given in a year?
    A. 24   B. 72   C. 144   D. 48

22._____

23. If Margot makes $34,000 per year and she works 40 hours per week for all 52 weeks, what is her hourly rate?
    A. $16.34/hour   B. $17.00/hour C. $15.54/hour D. $13.23/hour

23._____

24. How many dimes are there in $175.00?
    A. 175   B. 1,750   C. 3,500   D. 17,500

24._____

25. If Janey is three times as old as Emily, and Emily is 3, how old is Janey?
    A. 6   B. 9   C. 12   D. 15

25._____

KEY (CORRECT ANSWERS)

1.	C	11.	B
2.	D	12.	A
3.	A	13.	D
4.	B	14.	B
5.	B	15.	A
6.	C	16.	C
7.	A	17.	A
8.	B	18.	C
9.	C	19.	B
10.	A	20.	A

21.	B
22.	C
23.	A
24.	B
25.	B

TEST 2

DIRECTIONS: Each question or incomplete statement is followed by several suggested answers or completions. Select the one that BEST answers the question or completes the statement. *PRINT THE LETTER OF THE CORRECT ANSWER IN THE SPACE AT THE RIGHT.*

Questions 1-6.

DIRECTIONS: Questions 1 through 6 are to be answered on the basis of the following information.

item	name of item to be ordered
quantity	minimum number that can be ordered
beginning amount	amount in stock at start of month
amount received	amount receiving during month
ending amount	amount in stock at end of month
amount used	amount used during month
amount to order	will need at least as much of each item as used in the previous month
unit price	cost of each unit of an item
total price	total price for the order

Item	Quantity	Beginning	Received	Ending	Amount Used	Amount to Order	Unit Price	Total Price
Pens	10	22	10	8	24	20	$0.11	$2.20
Spiral notebooks	8	30	13	12			$0.25	
Binder clips	2 boxes	3 boxes	1 box	1 box			$1.79	
Sticky notes	3 packs	12 packs	4 packs	2 packs			$1.29	
Dry erase markers	1 pack (dozen)	34 markers	8 markers	40 markers			$16.49	
Ink cartridges (printer)	1 cartridge	3 cartridges	1 cartridge	2 cartridges			$79.99	
Folders	10 folders	25 folders	15 folders	10 folders			$1.08	

1. How many packs of sticky notes were used during the month?   1.____
    A. 16   B. 10   C. 12   D. 14

2. How many folders need to be ordered for next month?   2.____
    A. 15   B. 20   C. 30   D. 40

3. What is the total price of notebooks that you will need to order?   3.____
    A. $6.00   B. $0.25   C. $4.50   D. $2.75

4. Which of the following will you spend the second most money on?   4.____
    A. Ink cartridges   B. Dry erase markers
    C. Sticky notes   D. Binder clips

5. How many packs of dry erase markers should you order?   5.____
    A. 1   B. 8   C. 12   D. 0

6. What will be the total price of the file folders you order?   6.____
   A. $20.16   B. $2.16   C. $1.08   D. $4.32

Questions 7-11.

DIRECTIONS: Questions 7 through 11 are to be answered on the basis of the following table.

Number of Car Accidents, By Location and Cause, for 2014						
	Location 1		Location 2		Location 3	
Cause	Number	Percent	Number	Percent	Number	Percent
Severe Weather	10		25		30	
Excessive Speeding	20	40	5		10	
Impaired Driving	15		15	25	8	
Miscellaneous	5		15		2	4
TOTALS	50	100	60	100	50	100

7. Which of the following is the third highest cause of accidents for all three   7.____
   locations?
   A. Severe Weather   B. Impaired Driving
   C. Miscellaneous   D. Excessive Speeding

8. The average number of Severe Weather accidents per week at Location 3   8.____
   for the year (52 weeks) was MOST NEARLY
   A. 0.57   B. 30   C. 1   D. 1.25

9. Which location had the LARGEST percentage of accidents caused by   9.____
   Impaired Driving?
   A. 1   B. 2   C. 3   D. Both A and B

10. If one-third of the accidents at all three locations resulted in at least one   10.____
    fatality, what is the LEAST amount of deaths caused by accidents last year?
    A. 60   B. 106   C. 66   D. 53

11. What is the percentage of accidents caused by miscellaneous means from   11.____
    all three locations in 2014?
    A. 5%   B. 10%   C. 13%   D. 25%

12. How many pairs of the following groups of letters are exactly alike?   12.____
    ACDOBJ   ACDBOJ
    HEWBWR   HEWRWB
    DEERVS   DEERVS
    BRFQSX   BRFQSX
    WEYRVB   WEYRVB
    SPQRZA   SQRPZA

    A. 2   B. 3   C. 4   D. 5

Questions 13-19.

DIRECTIONS: Questions 13 through 19 are to be answered on the basis of the following information.

In 2012, the most current information on the American population was finished. The information was compiled by 200 volunteers in each of the 50 states. The territory of Puerto Rico, a sovereign of the United States, had 25 people assigned to compile data. In February of 2010, volunteers in each state and sovereign began collecting information. In Puerto Rico, data collection finished by January 31st, 2011, while work in the United States was completed on June 30, 2012. Each volunteer gathered data on the population of their state or sovereign. When the information was compiled, volunteers sent reports to the nation's capital, Washington, D.C. Each volunteer worked 20 hours per month and put together 10 reports per month. After the data was compiled in total, 50 people reviewed the data and worked from January 2012 to December 2012.

13. How many reports were generated from February 2010 to April 2010 in Illinois and Ohio?　　　　　　　　　　　　　　　　　　　　　　　　　13._____
　　　A. 3,000　　　　　B. 6,000　　　　　C. 12,000　　　　　D. 15,000

14. How many volunteers in total collected population data in January 2012?　　14._____
　　　A. 10,000　　　　B. 2,000　　　　C. 225　　　　D. 200

15. How many reports were put together in May 2012?　　　　　　　　　　　15._____
　　　A. 2,000　　　　B. 50,000　　　　C. 100,000　　　　D. 100,250

16. How many hours did the Puerto Rican volunteers work in the fall (September-November)?　　　　　　　　　　　　　　　　　　　　　　16._____
　　　A. 60　　　　　B. 500　　　　　C. 1,500　　　　　D. 0

17. How many workers were compiling or reviewing data in July 2012?　　　　17._____
　　　A. 25　　　　　B. 50　　　　　C. 200　　　　　D. 250

18. What was the total amount of hours worked by Nevada volunteers in July 2010?　18._____
　　　A. 500　　　　　B. 4,000　　　　　C. 4,500　　　　　D. 5,000

19. How many reviewers worked in January 2013?　　　　　　　　　　　　　19._____
　　　A. 75　　　　　B. 50　　　　　C. 0　　　　　D. 25

20. John has to file 10 documents per shelf. How many documents would it take for John to fill 40 shelves?　　　　　　　　　　　　　　　　　　20._____
　　　A. 40　　　　　B. 400　　　　　C. 4,500　　　　　D. 5,000

21. Jill wants to travel from New York City to Los Angeles by bike, which is approximately 2,772 miles. How many miles per day would Jill need to average if she wanted to complete the trip in 4 weeks?　　　　　　　21._____
　　　A. 100　　　　　B. 89　　　　　C. 99　　　　　D. 94

22. If there are 24 CPU's and only 7 monitors, how many more monitors do
    you need to have the same amount of monitors as CPU's?
    A. Not enough information   B. 17
    C. 31   D. 0

    22._____

23. If Gerry works 5 days a week and 8 hours each day, and John works 3 days
    a week and 10 hours each day, how many more hours per year will Gerry work
    than John?
    A. They work the same amount of hours.
    B. 450
    C. 520
    D. 832

    23._____

24. Jimmy gets transferred to a new office. The new office has 25 employees,
    but only 16 are there due to a blizzard. How many coworkers was Jimmy able
    to meet on his first day?
    A. 16   B. 25   C. 9   D. 7

    24._____

25. If you do a fundraiser for charities in your area and raise $500 total, how
    much would you give to each charity if you were donating equal amounts to 3
    of them?
    A. $250.00   B. $167.77   C. $50.00   D. $111.11

    25._____

KEY (CORRECT ANSWERS)

1.	D		11.	C
2.	B		12.	B
3.	A		13.	C
4.	C		14.	A
5.	D		15.	C
6.	B		16.	C
7.	D		17.	B
8.	A		18.	B
9.	A		19.	C
10.	D		20.	B

21.	C
22.	B
23.	C
24.	A
25.	B

TEST 3

DIRECTIONS: Each question or incomplete statement is followed by several suggested answers or completions. Select the one that BEST answers the question or completes the statement. *PRINT THE LETTER OF THE CORRECT ANSWER IN THE SPACE AT THE RIGHT.*

Questions 1-3.

DIRECTIONS: In answering Questions 1 through 3, choose the correctly spelled word.

1. A. allusion   B. alusion   C. allusien   D. allution   1.____

2. A. altitude   B. alltitude   C. atlitude   D. altlitude   2.____

3. A. althogh   B. allthough   C. althrough   D. although   3.____

Questions 4-9.

DIRECTIONS: In answering Questions 4 through 9, choose the answer that BEST completes the analogy.

4. Odometer is to mileage as compass is to   4.____
    A. speed   B. needle   C. hiking   D. direction

5. Marathon is to race as hibernation is to   5.____
    A. winter   B. dream   C. sleep   D. bear

6. Cup is to coffee as bowl is to   6.____
    A. dish   B. spoon   C. food   D. soup

7. Flow is to river as stagnant is to   7.____
    A. pool   B. rain   C. stream   D. canal

8. Paw is to cat as hoof is to   8.____
    A. lamb   B. horse   C. lion   D. elephant

9. Architect is to building as sculptor is to   9.____
    A. museum   B. chisel   C. stone   D. statue

Questions 10-14.

DIRECTIONS: Questions 10 through 14 are to be answered on the basis of the following graph.

Population of Carroll City Broken Down by Age and Gender (in Thousands)			
Age	Female	Male	Total
Under 15	60	60	120
15-23		22	
24-33		20	44
34-43	13	18	31
44-53	20		67
64 and Over	65	65	130
TOTAL	230	232	462

10. How many people in the city are between the ages of 15-23?
    A. 70   B. 46,000   C. 70,000   D. 225,000

10.____

11. Approximately what percentage of the total population of the city was female aged 24-33?
    A. 10%   B. 5%   C. 15%   D. 25%

11.____

12. If 33% of the males have a job and 55% of females don't have a job, which of the following statements is TRUE?
    A. Males have approximately 2,600 more jobs than females.
    B. Females have approximately 49,000 more jobs than males.
    C. Females have approximately 26,000 more jobs than males.
    D. None of the above statements are true.

12.____

13. How many females between the ages of 15-23 live in Carroll City?
    A. 67,000   B. 24,000   C. 48,000   D. 91,000

13.____

14. Assume all males 44-53 living in Carroll City are employed. If two-thirds of males age 44-53 work jobs outside of Carroll City, how many work within city limits?
    A. 31,333
    B. 15,667
    C. 47,000
    D. Cannot answer the question with the information provided

14.____

Questions 15-16.

DIRECTIONS: Questions 15 and 16 are labeled as shown. Alphabetize them for filing. Choose the answer that correctly shows the order.

15. (1) AED
    (2) OOS
    (3) FOA
    (4) DOM
    (5) COB

    A. 2-5-4-3-2   B. 1-4-5-2-3   C. 1-5-4-2-3   D. 1-5-4-3-2

15._____

16. Alphabetize the names of the people. Last names are given last.
    (1) Lindsey Jamestown
    (2) Jane Alberta
    (3) Ally Jamestown
    (4) Allison Johnston
    (5) Lyle Moreno

    A. 2-1-3-4-5   B. 3-4-2-1-5   C. 2-3-1-4-5   D. 4-3-2-1-5

16._____

17. Which of the following words is misspelled?
    A. disgust   B. whisper
    C. locale   D. none of the above

17._____

Questions 18-21.

DIRECTIONS: Questions 18 through 21 are to be answered on the basis of the following list of employees.

Robertson, Aaron
Bacon, Gina
Jerimiah, Trace
Gillette, Stanley
Jacks, Sharon

18. Which employee name would come in third in alphabetized list?
    A. Robertson, Aaron   B. Jerimiah, Trace
    C. Gillette, Stanley   D. Jacks, Sharon

18._____

19. Which employee's first name starts with the letter in the alphabet that is five letters after the first letter of their last name?
    A. Jerimiah, Trace   B. Bacon, Gina
    C. Jacks, Sharon   D. Gillette, Stanley

19._____

20. How many employees have last names that are exactly five letters long?
    A. 1   B. 2   C. 3   D. 4

20._____

21. How many of the employees have either a first or last name that starts
with the letter "G"?
    A. 1   B. 2   C. 4   D. 5

21.____

Questions 22-25.

DIRECTIONS: Questions 22 through 25 are to be answered on the basis of the following chart.

Bicycle Sales (Model #34JA32)							
Country	May	June	July	August	September	October	Total
Germany	34	47	45	54	56	60	296
Britain	40	44	36	47	47	46	260
Ireland	37	32	32	32	34	33	200
Portugal	14	14	14	16	17	14	89
Italy	29	29	28	31	29	31	177
Belgium	22	24	24	26	25	23	144
Total	176	198	179	206	208	207	1166

22. What percentage of the overall total was sold to the German importer?
    A. 25.3%   B. 22%   C. 24.1%   D. 23%

22.____

23. What percentage of the overall total was sold in September?
    A. 24.1%   B. 25.6%   C. 17.9%   D. 24.6%

23.____

24. What is the average number of units per month imported into Belgium over
the first four months shown?
    A. 26   B. 20   C. 24   D. 31

24.____

25. If you look at the three smallest importers, what is their total import
percentage?
    A. 35.1%   B. 37.1%   C. 40%   D. 28%

25.____

KEY (CORRECT ANSWERS)

1.	A		11.	B
2.	A		12.	C
3.	D		13.	C
4.	D		14.	B
5.	C		15.	D
6.	D		16.	C
7.	A		17.	D
8.	B		18.	D
9.	D		19.	B
10.	C		20.	B

21.	B
22.	A
23.	C
24.	C
25.	A

TEST 4

DIRECTIONS: Each question or incomplete statement is followed by several suggested answers or completions. Select the one that BEST answers the question or completes the statement. *PRINT THE LETTER OF THE CORRECT ANSWER IN THE SPACE AT THE RIGHT.*

Questions 1-6.

DIRECTIONS: In answering Questions 1 through 6, choose the sentence that represents the BEST example of English grammar.

1. A. Joey and me want to go on a vacation next week.   1.____
    B. Gary told Jim he would need to take some time off.
    C. If turning six years old, Jim's uncle would teach Spanish to him.
    D. Fax a copy of your resume to Ms. Perez and me.

2. A. Jerry stood in line for almost two hours.   2.____
    B. The reaction to my engagement was less exciting than I thought it would be.
    C. Carlos and me have done great work on this project.
    D. Two parts of the speech needs to be revised before tomorrow.

3. A. Arriving home, the alarm was tripped.   3.____
    B. Jonny is regarded as a stand up guy, a responsible parent, and he doesn't give up until a task is finished.
    C. Each employee must submit a drug test each month.
    D. One of the documents was incinerated in the explosion.

4. A. As soon as my parents get home, I told them I finished all of my chores.   4.____
    B. I asked my teacher to send me my missing work, check my absences, and how did I do on my test.
    C. Matt attempted to keep it concealed from Jenny and me.
    D. If Mary or him cannot get work done on time, I will have to split them up.

5. A. Driving to work, the traffic report warned him of an accident on Highway 47.   5.____
    B. Jimmy has performed well this season.
    C. Since finishing her degree, several job offers have been given to Cam.
    D. Our boss is creating unstable conditions for we employees.

6. A. The thief was described as a tall man with a wiry mustache weighing approximately 150 pounds.   6.____
    B. She gave Patrick and I some more time to finish our work.
    C. One of the books that he ordered was damaged in shipping.
    D. While talking on the rotary phone, the car Jim was driving skidded off the road.

2 (#4)

Questions 7-9.

DIRECTIONS: Questions 7 through 9 are to be answered on the basis of the following graph.

Ice Lake Frozen Flight (2002-2013)		
Year	Number of Participants	Temperature (Fahrenheit)
2002	22	4°
2003	50	33°
2004	69	18°
2005	104	22°
2006	108	24°
2007	288	33°
2008	173	9°
2009	598	39°
2010	698	26°
2011	696	30°
2012	777	28°
2013	578	32°

7. Which two year span had the LARGEST difference between temperatures?   7._____
   A. 2002 and 2003   B. 2011 and 2012
   C. 2008 and 2009   D. 2003 and 2004

8. How many total people participated in the years after the temperature   8._____
reached at least 29°?
   A. 2,295   B. 1,717   C. 2,210   D. 4,543

9. In 2007, the event saw 288 participants, while in 2008 that number   9._____
dropped to 173. Which of the following reasons BEST explains the drop in
participants?
   A. The event had not been going on that long and people didn't know about
      it.
   B. The lake water wasn't cold enough to have people jump in.
   C. The temperature was too cold for many people who would have normally
      participated.
   D. None of the above reasons explain the drop in participants.

10. In the following list of numbers, how many times does 4 come just after 2   10._____
when 2 comes just after an odd number?
2365247653898632488572486392424
   A. 2   B. 3   C. 4   D. 5

11. Which choice below lists the letter that is as far after B as S is after N in   11._____
the alphabet?
   A. G   B. H   C. I   D. J

Questions 12-15.

DIRECTIONS: Questions 12 through 15 are to be answered on the basis of the following directory and list of changes.

Directory		
Name	Emp. Type	Position
Julie Taylor	Warehouse	Packer
James King	Office	Administrative Assistant
John Williams	Office	Salesperson
Ray Moore	Warehouse	Maintenance
Kathleen Byrne	Warehouse	Supervisor
Amy Jones	Office	Salesperson
Paul Jonas	Office	Salesperson
Lisa Wong	Warehouse	Loader
Eugene Lee	Office	Accountant
Bruce Lavine	Office	Manager
Adam Gates	Warehouse	Packer
Will Suter	Warehouse	Packer
Gary Lorper	Office	Accountant
Jon Adams	Office	Salesperson
Susannah Harper	Office	Salesperson

Directory Updates:
- Employee e-mail address will adhere to the following guidelines: lastnamefirstname@apexindustries.com (ex. Susannah Harper is harpersusannah@apexindustries.com). Currently, employees in the warehouse share one e-mail, distribution@apexindustries.com.
- The "Loader" position was now be referred to as "Specialist I"
- Adam Gates has accepted a Supervisor position within the Warehouse and is no longer a Packer. All warehouses employees report to the two Supervisors and all office employees report to the Manager.

12. Amy Jones tried to send an e-mail to Adam Gates, but it wouldn't send. Which of the following offers the BEST explanation?
    A. Amy put Adam's first name first and then his last name.
    B. Adam doesn't check his e-mail, so he wouldn't know if he received the e-mail or not.
    C. Adam does not have his own e-mail.
    D. Office employees are not allowed to send e-mails to each other.

12.____

13. How many Packers currently work for Apex Industries?
    A. 2   B. 3   C. 4   D. 5

13.____

14. What position does Lisa Wong currently hold?
    A. Specialist I   B. Secretary
    C. Administrative Assistant   D. Loader

14.____

15. If an employee wanted to contact the office manager, which of the
    following e-mails should the e-mail be sent to?
    A. officemanager@apexindustries.com
    B. brucelavine@apexindustries.com
    C. lavinebruce@apexindustries.com
    D. distribution@apexindustries.com

15.____

Questions 16-19.

DIRECTIONS: In answering Questions 16 through 19, compare the three names, numbers or
            addresses.

16. Smiley Yarnell   Smiley Yarnel   Smily Yarnell
    A. All three are exactly alike.
    B. The first and second are exactly alike.
    C. The second and third are exactly alike.
    D. All three are different.

16.____

17. 1583 Theater Drive   1583 Theater Drive   1583 Theatre Drive
    A. All three are exactly alike.
    B. The first and second are exactly alike.
    C. The second and third are exactly alike.
    D. All three are different.

17.____

18. 3341893212   3341893212   3341893212
    A. All three are exactly alike.
    B. The first and second are exactly alike.
    C. The second and third are exactly alike.
    D. All three are different.

18.____

19. Douglass Watkins   Douglas Watkins   Douglass Watkins
    A. All three are exactly alike.
    B. The first and third are exactly alike.
    C. The second and third are exactly alike.
    D. All three are different.

19.____

Questions 20-24.

DIRECTIONS: In answering Questions 20 through 24, you will be presented with a word.
            Choose the synonym that BEST represents the word in question.

20. Flexible
    A. delicate   B. inflammable C. strong   D. pliable

20.____

21. Alternative
    A. choice   B. moderate C. lazy   D. value

21.____

22. Corroborate
    A. examine   B. explain   C. verify   D. explain   22._____

23. Respiration
    A. recovery   B. breathing   C. sweating   D. selfish   23._____

24. Negligent
    A. lazy   B. moderate   C. hopeless   D. lax   24._____

25. Plumber is to Wrench as Painter is to   25._____
    A. pipe   B. shop   C. hammer   D. brush

KEY (CORRECT ANSWERS)

1.	D		11.	A
2.	A		12.	C
3.	D		13.	A
4.	C		14.	A
5.	B		15.	C
6.	C		16.	D
7.	C		17.	B
8.	B		18.	A
9.	C		19.	B
10.	C		20.	D

21.	A
22.	C
23.	B
24.	D
25.	D

NAME and NUMBER COMPARISONS

COMMENTARY

This test seeks to measure your ability and disposition to do a job carefully and accurately, your attention to exactness and preciseness of detail, your alertness and versatility in discerning similarities and differences between things, and your power in systematically handling written language symbols.

It is actually a test of your ability to do academic and/or clerical work, using the basic elements of verbal (qualitative) and mathematical (quantitative) learning – words _and_ numbers.

EXAMINATION SECTION
TEST 1

Tests 1-2

DIRECTIONS: Questions 1 through 6 consist of sets of names and addresses. In each question, the name and address in Column II should be an exact copy of the name and address in Column I. _PRINT IN THE SPACE AT THE RIGHT THE LETTER:_
  A.   if there is a mistake only in the name
  B.   if there is a mistake only in the address
  C.   if there is a mistake in both name and address
  D.   if there is no mistake in either name or address

SAMPLE:

Michael Filbert   Michael Filbert
456 Reade Street   645 Reade Street
New York, N.Y. 10013   New York, N.Y. 10013

Since there is a mistake only in the address, the answer is B.

1. Esta Wong   Esta Wang   1.____
   141 West 68 St.   141 West 68 St.
   New York, N.Y. 10023   New York, N.Y. 10023

2. Dr. Alberto Grosso   Dr. Alberto Grosso   2.____
   3475 12th Avenue   3475 12th Avenue
   Brooklyn, N.Y. 11218   Brooklyn, N.Y. 11218

3. Mrs. Ruth Bortlas   Ms. Ruth Bortlas   3.____
   482 Theresa Ct.   482 Theresa Ct.
   Far Rockaway, N.Y. 11691   Far Rockaway, N.Y. 11169

4. Mr. and Mrs. Howard Fox   Mr. and Mrs. Howard Fox   4.____
   2301 Sedgwick Ave.   231 Sedgwick Ave.
   Bronx, N.Y. 10468   Bronx, N.Y. 10468

5. Miss Marjorie Black   Miss Margorie Black   5.____
   223 East 23 Street   223 East 23 Street
   New York, N.Y. 10010   New York, N.Y. 10010

6. Michelle Herman
    806 Valley Rd.
    Old Tappan, N.J. 07675

    Michelle Hermann
    806 Valley Dr.
    Old Tappan, N.J. 07675

6.____

─────────

KEY (CORRECT ANSWERS)

1. A
2. D
3. C
4. B
5. A
6. C

─────────

TEST 2

DIRECTIONS: Questions 1 through 6 consist of sets of names and addresses. In each question, the name and address in Column II should be an exact copy of the name and address in Column I. *PRINT IN THE SPACE AT THE RIGHT THE LETTER:*

A. if there is a mistake only in the name
B. if there is a mistake only in the address
C. if there is a mistake in both name and address
D. if there is no mistake in either name or address

	Column I	Column II	
1.	Ms. Joan Kelly 313 Franklin Ave. Brooklyn, N.Y. 11202	Ms. Joan Kielly 318 Franklin Ave. Brooklyn, N.Y. 11202	1.____
2.	Mrs. Eileen Engel 47-24 86 Road Queens, N.Y. 11122	Mrs. Ellen Engel 47-24 86 Road Queens, N.Y. 11122	2.____
3.	Marcia Michaels 213 E. 81 St. New York, N.Y. 10012	Marcia Michaels 213 E. 81 St. New York, N.Y. 10012	3.____
4.	Rev. Edward J. Smyth 1401 Brandeis Street San Francisco, Calif. 96201	Rev. Edward J. Smyth 1401 Brandies Street San Francisco, Calif. 96201	4.____
5.	Alicia Rodriguez 24-68 81 St. Elmhurst, N.Y. 11122	Alicia Rodriquez 2468 81 St. Elmhurst, N.Y. 11122	5.____
6.	Ernest Eisemann 21 Columbia St. New York, N.Y. 10007	Ernest Eisermann 21 Columbia St. New York, N.Y. 10007	6.____

KEY (CORRECT ANSWERS)

1. C
2. A
3. D
4. B
5. C
6. A

TEST 3

DIRECTIONS: Questions 1 through 8 consist of names, locations and telephone numbers. In each question, the name, location and number in Column II should be an exact copy of the name, location and number in Column I. *PRINT IN THE SPACE AT THE RIGHT THE LETTER:*

A. if there is a mistake in one line only
B. if there is a mistake in two lines only
C. if there is a mistake in three lines only
D. if there are no mistakes in any of the lines

1. Ruth Lang
   EAM Bldg., Room C101
   625-2000, ext. 765

   Ruth Lang
   EAM Bldg., Room C110
   625-2000, ext. 765

   1.____

2. Anne Marie Ionozzi
   Investigations, Room 827
   576-4000, ext. 832

   Anna Marie Ionozzi
   Investigation, Room 827
   566-4000, ext. 832

   2.____

3. Willard Jameson
   Fm C Bldg. Room 687
   454-3010

   Willard Jamieson
   Fm C Bldg. Room 687
   454-3010

   3.____

4. Joanne Zimmermann
   Bldg. SW, Room 314
   532-4601

   Joanne Zimmermann
   Bldg. SW, Room 314
   532-4601

   4.____

5. Carlyle Whetstone
   Payroll Division-A, Room 212A
   262-5000, ext. 471

   Caryle Whetstone
   Payroll Division-A, Room 212A
   262-5000, ext. 417

   5.____

6. Kenneth Chiang
   Legal Council, Room 9745
   (201) 416-9100, ext. 17

   Kenneth Chiang
   Legal Counsel, Room 9745
   (201) 416-9100, ext. 17

   6.____

7. Ethel Koenig
   Personnel Services Div, Rm 433
   635-7572

   Ethel Hoenig
   Personal Services Div, Rm 433
   635-7527

   7.____

8. Joyce Ehrhardt
   Office of Administrator, Rm W56
   387-8706

   Joyce Ehrhart
   Office of Administrator, Rm W56
   387-7806

   8.____

KEY (CORRECT ANSWERS)

1. A
2. C
3. A
4. D
5. B

6. A
7. C
8. B

———

TEST 4

DIRECTIONS: Each of questions 1 through 10 gives the identification number and name of a person who has received treatment at a certain hospital. You are to choose the option (A, B, C or D) which has EXACTLY the same number and name as those given in the question.

SAMPLE:
123765 Frank Y. Jones
- A. 123675 Frank Y. Jones
- B. 123765 Frank T. Jones
- C. 123765 Frank Y. Johns
- D. 123765 Frank Y. Jones

The correct answer is D, because it is the only option showing the identification number and name exactly as they are in the sample question.

1. 754898 Diane Malloy

- A. 745898 Diane Malloy
- B. 754898 Dion Malloy
- C. 754898 Diane Malloy
- D. 754898 Diane Maloy

1.____

2. 661818 Ferdinand Figueroa

- A. 661818 Ferdinand Figeuroa
- B. 661618 Ferdinand Figueroa
- C. 661818 Ferdnand Figueroa
- D. 661818 Ferdinand Figueroa

2.____

3. 100101 Norman D. Braustein

- A. 100101 Norman D. Braustein
- B. 101001 Norman D. Braustein
- C. 100101 Norman P. Braustien
- D. 100101 Norman D. Bruastein

3.____

4. 838696 Robert Kittredge

- A. 838969 Robert Kittredge
- B. 838696 Robert Kittredge
- C. 388696 Robert Kittredge
- D. 838696 Robert Kittridge

4.____

5. 243716 Abraham Soletsky

- A. 243716 Abrahm Soletsky
- B. 243716 Abraham Solestky
- C. 243176 Abraham Soletsky
- D. 243716 Abraham Soletsky

5.____

6. 981121 Phillip M. Maas

    A. 981121 Phillip M. Mass
    B. 981211 Phillip M. Maas
    C. 981121 Phillip M. Maas
    D. 981121 Phillip N. Maas

6.____

7. 786556 George Macalusso

    A. 785656 George Macalusso
    B. 786556 George Macalusso
    C. 786556 George Maculusso
    D. 786556 George Macluasso

7.____

8. 639472 Eugene Weber

    A. 639472 Eugene Weber
    B. 639472 Eugene Webre
    C. 693472 Eugene Weber
    D. 639742 Eugene Weber

8.____

9. 724936 John J. Lomonaco

    A. 724936 John J. Lomanoco
    B. 724396 John L. Lomonaco
    C. 724936 John J. Lomonaco
    D. 724936 John J. Lamonaco

9.____

10. 899868 Michael Schnitzer

    A. 899868 Micheal Schnitzer
    B. 898968 Michael Schnizter
    C. 899688 Michael Schnitzer
    D. 899868 Michael Schnitzer

10.____

———

KEY (CORRECT ANSWERS)

1.	C		6.	C
2.	D		7.	B
3.	A		8.	A
4.	B		9.	C
5.	D		10.	D

———

EXAMINATION SECTION
TEST 1

DIRECTIONS: Each question or incomplete statement is followed by several suggested answers or completions. Select the one that BEST answers the question or completes the statement. *PRINT THE LETTER OF THE CORRECT ANSWER IN THE SPACE AT THE RIGHT.*

1. Which of the following sentences is punctuated INCORRECTLY?   1.____

    A. Johnson said, "One tiny virus, Blanche, can multiply so fast that it will become 200 viruses in 25 minutes."
    B. With economic pressures hitting them from all sides, American farmers have become the weak link in the food chain.
    C. The degree to which this is true, of course, depends on the personalities of the people involved, the subject matter, and the atmosphere in general.
    D. "What loneliness, asked George Eliot, is more lonely than distrust?"

2. Which of the following sentences is punctuated INCORRECTLY?   2.____

    A. Based on past experiences, do you expect the plumber to show up late, not have the right parts, and overcharge you.
    B. When polled, however, the participants were most concerned that it be convenient.
    C. No one mentioned the flavor of the coffee, and no one seemed to care that china was used instead of plastic.
    D. As we said before, sometimes people view others as things; they don't see them as living, breathing beings like themselves.

3. Convention members travelled here from Kingston New York Pittsfield Massachusetts   3.____
    Bennington Vermont and Hartford Connecticut.
    How many commas should there be in the above sentence?

    A. 3   B. 4   C. 5   D. 6

4. Of the two speakers the one who spoke about human rights is more famous and more   4.____
    humble.
    How many commas should there be in the above sentence?

    A. 1   B. 2   C. 3   D. 4

5. Which sentence is punctuated INCORRECTLY?   5.____

    A. Five people voted no; two voted yes; one person abstained.
    B. Well, consider what has been said here today, but we won't make any promises.
    C. Anthropologists divide history into three major periods: the Stone Age, the Bronze Age, and the Iron Age.
    D. Therefore, we may create a stereotype about people who are unsuccessful; we may see them as lazy, unintelligent, or afraid of success.

6. Which sentence is punctuated INCORRECTLY?   6.____

    A. Studies have found that the unpredictability of customer behavior can lead to a great deal of stress, particularly if the behavior is unpleasant or if the employee has little control over it.

B. If this degree of emotion and variation can occur in spectator sports, imagine the role that perceptions can play when there are real stakes involved.
C. At other times, however hidden expectations may sabotage or severely damage an encounter without anyone knowing what happened.
D. There are usually four issues to look for in a conflict: differences in values, goals, methods, and facts.

Questions 7-10.

DIRECTIONS: Questions 7 through 10 test your ability to distinguish between words that sound alike but are spelled differently and have different meanings. In the following groups of sentences, one of the underlined words is used incorrectly.

7.   A. By accepting responsibility for their actions, managers promote trust.   7.____
     B. Dropping hints or making illusions to things that you would like changed sometimes leads to resentment.
     C. The entire unit loses respect for the manager and resents the reprimand.
     D. Many people are averse to confronting problems directly; they would rather avoid them.

8.   A. What does this say about the effect our expectations have on those we supervise?   8.____
     B. In an effort to save time between 9 A.M. and 1 P.M., the staff members devised their own interpretation of what was to be done on these forms.
     C. The task master's principal concern is for getting the work done; he or she is not concerned about the needs or interests of employees.
     D. The advisor's main objective was increasing Angela's ability to invest her capitol wisely.

9.   A. A typical problem is that people have to cope with the internal censer of their feelings.   9.____
     B. Sometimes, in their attempt to sound more learned, people speak in ways that are barely comprehensible.
     C. The council will meet next Friday to decide whether Abrams should continue as representative.
     D. His descent from grace was assured by that final word.

10. A. The doctor said that John's leg had to remain stationary or it would not heal properly.   10.____
     B. There is a city ordinance against parking too close to fire hydrants.
     C. Meyer's problem is that he is never discrete when talking about office politics.
     D. Mrs. Thatcher probably worked harder than any other British Prime Minister had ever worked.

Questions 11-20.

DIRECTIONS: For each of the following groups of sentences in Questions 11 through 20, select the sentence which is the BEST example of English usage and grammar.

11. A. She is a woman who, at age sixty, is distinctly attractive and cares about how they look.
    B. It was a seemingly impossible search, and no one knew the problems better than she.
    C. On the surface, they are all sweetness and light, but his morbid character is under it.
    D. The minicopier, designed to appeal to those who do business on the run like architects in the field or business travelers, weigh about four pounds.

11._____

12. A. Neither the administrators nor the union representative regret the decision to settle the disagreement.
    B. The plans which are made earlier this year were no longer being considered.
    C. I would have rode with him if I had known he was leaving at five.
    D. I don't know who she said had it.

12._____

13. A. Writing at a desk, the memo was handed to her for immediate attention.
    B. Carla didn't water Carl's plants this week, which she never does.
    C. Not only are they good workers, with excellent writing and speaking skills, and they get to the crux of any problem we hand them.
    D. We've noticed that this enthusiasm for undertaking new projects sometimes interferes with his attention to detail.

13._____

14. A. It's obvious that Nick offends people by being unruly, inattentive, and having no patience.
    B. Marcia told Genie that she would have to leave soon.
    C. Here are the papers you need to complete your investigation.
    D. Julio was startled by you're comment.

14._____

15. A. The new manager has done good since receiving her promotion, but her secretary has helped her a great deal.
    B. One of the personnel managers approached John and tells him that the client arrived unexpectedly.
    C. If somebody can supply us with the correct figures, they should do so immediately.
    D. Like zealots, advocates seek power because they want to influence the policies and actions of an organization.

15._____

16. A. Between you and me, Chris probably won't finish this assignment in time.
    B. Rounding the corner, the snack bar appeared before us.
    C. Parker's radical reputation made to the Supreme Court his appointment impossible.
    D. By the time we arrived, Marion finishes briefing James and returns to Hank's office.

16._____

17.
   A.   As we pointed out earlier, the critical determinant of the success of middle manag-   17.____
ers is their ability to communicate well with others.
   B.   The lecturer stated there wasn't no reason for bad supervision.
   C.   We are well aware whose at fault in this instance.
   D.   When planning important changes, it's often wise to seek the partic-
ipation of others because employees often have much valuable
ideas to offer.

18.
   A.   Joan had ought to throw out those old things that were damaged when the roof   18.____
leaked.
   B.   I spose he'll let us know what he's decided when he finally comes to
a decision.
   C.   Carmen was walking to work when she suddenly realized that she
had left her lunch on the table as she passed the market.
   D.   Are these enough plants for your new office?

19.
   A.   First move the lever forward, and then they should lift the ribbon casing before try-   19.____
ing to take it out.
   B.   Michael finished quickest than any other person in the office.
   C.   There is a special meeting for we committee members today at 4
p.m.
   D.   My husband is worried about our having to work overtime next
week.

20.
   A.   Another source of conflicts are individuals who possess very poor interpersonal   20.____
skills.
   B.   It is difficult for us to work with him on projects because these kinds
of people are not interested in team building.
   C.   Each of the departments was represented at the meeting.
   D.   Poor boy, he never should of past that truck on the right.

Questions 21-28.

DIRECTIONS: In Questions 21 through 28, there may be a problem with English grammar or
usage. If a problem does exist, select the letter that indicates the most effective change. If no problem exists, select choice A.

21.   He rushed her to the hospital and stayed with her, even though this took quite a bit of his   21.____
time, he didn't charge her anything.

   A.   No changes are necessary
   B.   Change even though to although
   C.   Change the first comma to a period and capitalize even
   D.   Change rushed to had rushed

22.   Waiting that appears unfairly feels longer than waiting that seems justified.   22.____

   A.   No changes are necessary
   B.   Change unfairly to unfair
   C.   Change appears to seems
   D.   Change longer to longest

23. May be you and the person who argued with you will be able to reach an agreement.   23._____

    A. No changes are necessary
    B. Change will be to were
    C. Change argued with to had an argument with
    D. Change May be to Maybe

24. Any one of them could of taken the file while you were having coffee.   24._____

    A. No changes are necessary
    B. Change any one to anyone
    C. Change of to have
    D. Change were having to were out having

25. While people get jobs or move from poverty level to better paying employment, they stop receiving benefits and start paying taxes.   25._____

    A. No changes are necessary
    B. Change While to As
    C. Change stop to will stop
    D. Change get to obtain

26. Maribeth's phone rang while talking to George about the possibility of their meeting Tom at three this afternoon.   26._____

    A. No changes are necessary
    B. Change their to her
    C. Move to George so that it follows Tom
    D. Change talking to she was talking

27. According to their father, Lisa is smarter than Chris, but Emily is the smartest of the three sisters.   27._____

    A. No changes are necessary
    B. Change their to her
    C. Change is to was
    D. Make two sentences, changing the second comma to a period and omitting but

28. Yesterday, Mark and he claim that Carl took Carol's ideas and used them inappropriately.   28._____

    A. No changes are necessary
    B. Change claim to claimed
    C. Change inappropriately to inappropriate
    D. Change Carol's to Carols'

Questions 29-34.

DIRECTIONS: For each group of sentences in Questions 29 through 34, select the choice that represents the BEST editing of the problem sentence.

29. The managers expected employees to be at their desks at all times, but they would always be late or leave unannounced.   29._____

A. The managers wanted employees to always be at their desks, but they would always be late or leave unannounced.
B. Although the managers expected employees to be at their desks no matter what came up, they would always be late and leave without telling anyone.
C. Although the managers expected employees to be at their desks at all times, the managers would always be late or leave without telling anyone.
D. The managers expected the employee to never leave their desks, but they would always be late or leave without telling anyone.

30. The one who is department manager he will call you to discuss the problem tomorrow morning at 10 A.M.   30._____

A. The one who is department manager will call you tomorrow morning at ten to discuss the problem.
B. The department manager will call you to discuss the problem tomorrow at 10 A.M.
C. Tomorrow morning at 10 A.M., the department manager will call you to discuss the problem.
D. Tomorrow morning the department manager will call you to discuss the problem.

31. A conference on child care in the workplace the $200 cost of which to attend may be prohibitive to childcare workers who earn less than that weekly.   31._____

A. A conference on child care in the workplace that costs $200 may be too expensive for childcare workers who earn less than that each week.
B. A conference on child care in the workplace, the cost of which to attend is $200, may be prohibitive to childcare workers who earn less than that weekly.
C. A conference on child care in the workplace who costs $200 may be too expensive for childcare workers who earn less than that a week.
D. A conference on child care in the workplace which costs $200 may be too expensive to childcare workers who earn less than that on a weekly basis.

32. In accordance with estimates recently made, there are 40,000 to 50,000 nuclear weapons in our world today.   32._____

A. Because of estimates recently, there are 40,000 to 50,000 nuclear weapons in the world today.
B. In accordance with estimates made recently, there are 40,000 to 50,000 nuclear weapons in the world today.
C. According to estimates made recently, there are 40,000 to 50,000 weapons in the world today.
D. According to recent estimates, there are 40,000 to 50,000 nuclear weapons in the world today.

33. Motivation is important in problem solving, but they say that excessive motivation can inhibit the creative process.   33._____

A. Motivation is important in problem solving, but, as they say, too much of it can inhibit the creative process.
B. Motivation is important in problem solving and excessive motivation will inhibit the creative process.
C. Motivation is important in problem solving, but excessive motivation can inhibit the creative process.

D. Motivation is important in problem solving because excessive motivation can inhibit the creative process.

34. In selecting the best option calls for consulting with all the people that are involved in it. 34.____

   A. In selecting the best option consulting with all the people concerned with it.
   B. Calling for the best option, we consulted all the affected people.
   C. We called all the people involved to select the best option.
   D. To be sure of selecting the best option, one should consult all the people involved.

35. There are a number of problems with the following letter. From the options below, select the version that is MOST in accordance with standard business style, tone, and form. 35.____

Dear Sir:

We are so sorry that we have had to backorder your order for 15,000 widgets and 2,300 whatzits for such a long time. We have been having incredibly bad luck lately. When your order first came in no one could get to it because my secretary was out with the flu and her replacement didn't know what she was doing, then there was the dock strike in Cucamonga which held things up for awhile, and then it just somehow got lost. We think it may have fallen behind the radiator.

We are happy to say that all these problems have been taken care of, we are caught up on supplies, and we should have the stuff to you soon, in the near future --about two weeks. You may not believe us after everything you've been through with us, but it's true.

We'll let you know as soon as we have a secure date for delivery. Thank you so much for continuing to do business with us after all the problems this probably has caused you.

Yours very sincerely,

Rob Barker

   A. Dear Sir:

   We are so sorry that we have had to backorder your order for 15,000 widgets and 2,300 whatzits. We have been having problems with staff lately and the dock strike hasn't helped anything.

   We are happy to say that all these problems have been taken care of. I've told my secretary to get right on it, and we should have the stuff to you soon. Thank you so much for continuing to do business with us after all the problems this must have caused you.

   We'll let you know as soon as we have a secure date for delivery.

   Sincerely,

   Rob Barker

B. Dear Sir:

We regret that we haven't been able to fill your order for 15,000 widgets and 2,300 whatzits in a timely fashion.

We'll let you know as soon as we have a secure date for delivery.

Sincerely,

Rob Barker

C. Dear Sir:

We are so very sorry that we haven't been able to fill your order for 15,000 widgets and 2,300 whatzits. We have been having incredibly bad luck lately, but things are much better now.

Thank you so much for bearing with us through all of this. We'll let you know as soon as we have a secure date for delivery.

Sincerely,

Rob Barker

D. Dear Sir:

We are very sorry that we haven't been able to fill your order for 15,000 widgets and 2,300 whatzits. Due to unforeseen difficulties, we have had to back-order your request. At this time, supplies have caught up to demand, and we foresee a delivery date within the next two weeks.

We'll let you know as soon as we have a secure date for delivery. Thank you for your patience.

Sincerely,

Rob Barker

———

KEY (CORRECT ANSWERS)

1.	D	16.	A
2.	A	17.	A
3.	B	18.	D
4.	A	19.	D
5.	B	20.	C
6.	C	21.	C
7.	B	22.	B
8.	D	23.	D
9.	A	24.	C
10.	C	25.	B
11.	B	26.	D
12.	D	27.	A
13.	D	28.	B
14.	C	29.	C
15.	D	30.	B

31.	A
32.	D
33.	C
34.	D
35.	D

READING COMPREHENSION
UNDERSTANDING AND INTERPRETING WRITTEN MATERIAL
EXAMINATION SECTION
TEST 1

DIRECTIONS: Each question or incomplete statement is followed by several suggested answers or completions. Select the one that BEST answers the question or completes the statement. *PRINT THE LETTER OF THE CORRECT ANSWER IN THE SPACE AT THE RIGHT.*

Questions 1-3.

DIRECTIONS: Questions 1 through 3 are to be answered SOLELY on the basis of the following statement.

The equipment in a mailroom may include a mail metering machine. This machine simultaneously stamps, postmarks, seals, and counts letters as fast as the operator can feed them. It can also print the proper postage directly on a gummed strip to be affixed to bulky items. It is equipped with a meter which is removed from the machine and sent to the postmaster to be set for a given number of stampings of any denomination. The setting of the meter must be paid for in advance. One of the advantages of metered mail is that it bypasses the cancellation operation and thereby facilitates handling by the post office. Mail metering also makes the pilfering of stamps impossible, but does not prevent the passage of personal mail in company envelopes through the meters unless there is established a rigid control or censorship over outgoing mail.

1. According to this statement, the postmaster   1.____

    A. is responsible for training new clerks in the use of mail metering machines
    B. usually recommends that both large and small firms adopt the use of mail metering machines
    C. is responsible for setting the meter to print a fixed number of stampings
    D. examines the mail metering machine to see that they are properly installed in the mailroom

2. According to this statement, the use of mail metering machines   2.____

    A. requires the employment of more clerks in a mailroom than does the use of postage stamps
    B. interferes with the handling of large quantities of outgoing mail
    C. does not prevent employees from sending their personal letters at company expense
    D. usually involves smaller expenditures for mailroom equipment than does the use of postage stamps

3. On the basis of this statement, it is MOST accurate to state that   3.____

    A. mail metering machines are often used for opening envelopes
    B. postage stamps are generally used when bulky packages are to be mailed
    C. the use of metered mail tends to interfere with rapid mail handling by the post office
    D. mail metering machines can seal and count letters at the same time

Questions 4-5.

DIRECTIONS: Questions 4 and 5 are to be answered SOLELY on the basis of the following statement.

Forms are printed sheets of paper on which information is to be entered. While what is printed on the form is most important, the kind of paper used in making the form is also important. The kind of paper should be selected with regard to the use to which the form will be subjected. Printing a form on an unnecessarily expensive grade of papers is wasteful. On the other hand, using too cheap or flimsy a form can materially interfere with satisfactory performance of the work the form is being planned to do. Thus, a form printed on both sides normally requires a heavier paper than a form printed only on one side. Forms to be used as permanent records, or which are expected to have a very long life in files, requires a quality of paper which will not disintegrate or discolor with age. A form which will go through a great deal of handling requires a strong, tough paper, while thinness is a necessary qualification where the making of several copies of a form will be required.

4. According to this statement, the type of paper used for making forms   4._____

    A. should be chosen in accordance with the use to which the form will be put
    B. should be chosen before the type of printing to be used has been decided upon
    C. is as important as the information which is printed on it
    D. should be strong enough to be used for any purpose

5. According to this statement, forms that are   5._____

    A. printed on both sides are usually economical and desirable
    B. to be filed permanently should not deteriorate as time goes on
    C. expected to last for a long time should be handled carefully
    D. to be filed should not be printed on inexpensive paper

Questions 6-8.

DIRECTIONS: Questions 6 through 8 are to be answered SOLELY on the basis of the following paragraph.

The increase in the number of public documents in the last two centuries closely matches the increase in population in the United States. The great number of public documents has become a serious threat to their usefulness. It is necessary to have programs which will reduce the number of public documents that are kept and which will, at the same time, assure keeping those that have value. Such programs need a great deal of thought to have any success.

6. According to the above paragraph, public documents may be LESS useful if   6._____

    A. the files are open to the public
    B. the record room is too small
    C. the copying machine is operated only during normal working hours
    D. too many records are being kept

7. According to the above paragraph, the growth of the population in the United States has   7.____
matched the growth in the quantity of public documents for a period of MOST NEARLY
_____ years.

    A.   50   B.   100   C.   200   D.   300

8. According to the above paragraph, the increased number of public documents has made   8.____
it necessary to

    A.   find out which public documents are worth keeping
    B.   reduce the great number of public documents by decreasing government services
    C.   eliminate the copying of all original public documents
    D.   avoid all new copying devices

Questions 9-10.

DIRECTIONS: Questions 9 and 10 are to be answered SOLELY on the basis of the following
                  paragraph.

    The work goals of an agency can best be reached if the employees understand and
agree with these goals. One way to gain such understanding and agreement is for management to encourage and seriously consider suggestions from employees in the setting of
agency goals.

9. On the basis of the above paragraph, the BEST way to achieve the work goals of an   9.____
agency is to

    A.   make certain that employees work as hard as possible
    B.   study the organizational structure of the agency
    C.   encourage employees to think seriously about the agency's problems
    D.   stimulate employee understanding of the work goals

10. On the basis of the above paragraph, understanding and agreement with agency goals   10.____
can be gained by

    A.   allowing the employees to set agency goals
    B.   reaching agency goals quickly
    C.   legislative review of agency operations
    D.   employee participation in setting agency goals

Questions 11-13.

DIRECTIONS: Questions 11 through 13 are to be answered SOLELY on the basis of the fol-
                  lowing paragraph.

    In order to organize records properly, it is necessary to start from their very beginning
and trace each copy of the record to find out how it is used, how long it is used, and what may
finally be done with it. Although several copies of the record are made, one copy should be
marked as the copy of record. This is the formal legal copy, held to meet the requirements of
the law. The other copies may be retained for brief periods for reference purposes, but these
copies should not be kept after their usefulness as reference ends. There is another reason
for tracing records through the office and that is to determine how long it takes the copy of
record to reach the central file. The copy of record must not be kept longer than necessary by

the section of the office which has prepared it, but should be sent to the central file as soon as possible so that it can be available to the various sections of the office. The central file can make the copy of record available to the various sections of the office at an early date only if it arrives at the central file as quickly as possible. Just as soon as its immediate or active service period is ended, the copy of record should be removed from the central file and put into the inactive file in the office to be stored for whatever length of time may be necessary to meet legal requirements, and then destroyed.

11. According to the above paragraph, a reason for tracing records through an office is to   11.____

    A. determine how long the central file must keep the records
    B. organize records properly
    C. find out how many copies of each record are required
    D. identify the copy of record

12. According to the above paragraph, in order for the central file to have the copy of record   12.____
available as soon as possible for the various sections of the office, it is MOST important that the

    A. copy of record to be sent to the central file meets the requirements of the law
    B. copy of record is not kept in the inactive file too long
    C. section preparing the copy of record does not unduly delay in sending it to the central file
    D. central file does not keep the copy of record beyond its active service period

13. According to the above paragraph, the length of time a copy of a record is kept in the   13.____
inactive file of an office depends CHIEFLY on the

    A. requirements of the law
    B. length of time that is required to trace the copy of record through the office
    C. use that is made of the copy of record
    D. length of the period that the copy of record is used for reference purposes

Questions 14-16.

DIRECTIONS: Questions 14 through 16 are to be answered SOLELY on the basis of the following paragraph.

The office was once considered as nothing more than a focal point of internal and external correspondence. It was capable only of dispatching a few letters upon occasion and of preparing records of little practical value. Under such a concept, the vitality of the office force was impaired. Initiative became stagnant, and the lot of the office worker was not likely to be a happy one. However, under the new concept of office management, the possibilities of waste and mismanagement in office operation are now fully recognized, as are the possibilities for the modern office to assist in the direction and control of business operations. Fortunately, the modern concept of the office as a centralized service-rendering unit is gaining ever greater acceptance in today's complex business world, for without the modern office, the production wheels do not turn and the distribution of goods and services is not possible.

14. According to the above paragraph, the fundamental difference between the old and the new concept of the office is the change in the

14.____

    A. accepted functions of the office
    B. content and the value of the records kept
    C. office methods and systems
    D. vitality and morale of the office force

15. According to the above paragraph, an office operated today under the old concept of the office MOST likely would

15.____

    A. make older workers happy in their jobs
    B. be part of an old thriving business concern
    C. have a passive role in the conduct of a business enterprise
    D. attract workers who do not believe in modern methods

16. Of the following, the MOST important implication of the above paragraph is that a present-day business organization cannot function effectively without the

16.____

    A. use of modern office equipment
    B. participation and cooperation of the office
    C. continued modernization of office procedures
    D. employment of office workers with skill and initiative

Questions 17-20.

DIRECTIONS: Questions 17 through 20 are to be answered SOLELY on the basis of the following paragraph.

    A report is frequently ineffective because the person writing it is not fully acquainted with all the necessary details before he actually starts to construct the report. All details pertaining to the subject should be known before the report is started. If the essential facts are not known, they should be investigated. It is wise to have essential facts written down rather than to depend too much on memory, especially if the facts pertain to such matters as amounts, dates, names of persons, or other specific data. When the necessary information has been gathered, the general plan and content of the report should be thought out before the writing is actually begun. A person with little or no experience in writing reports may find that it is wise to make a brief outline. Persons with more experience should not need a written outline, but they should make mental notes of the steps they are to follow. If writing reports without dictation is a regular part of an office worker's duties, he should set aside a certain time during the day when he is least likely to be interrupted. That may be difficult, but in most offices there are certain times in the day when the callers, telephone calls, and other interruptions are not numerous. During those times, it is best to write reports that need undivided concentration. Reports that are written amid a series of interruptions may be poorly done.

17. Before starting to write an effective report, it is necessary to

17.____

    A. memorize all specific information
    B. disregard ambiguous data
    C. know all pertinent information
    D. develop a general plan

18. Reports dealing with complex and difficult material should be

    A. prepared and written by the supervisor of the unit
    B. written when there is the least chance of interruption
    C. prepared and written as part of regular office routine
    D. outlined and then dictated

18.____

19. According to the paragraph, employees with no prior familiarity in writing reports may find it helpful to

    A. prepare a brief outline
    B. mentally prepare a synopsis of the report's content
    C. have a fellow employee help in writing the report
    D. consult previous reports

19.____

20. In writing a report, needed information which is unclear should be

    A. disregarded   B. memorized
    C. investigated   D. gathered

20.____

Questions 21-25.

DIRECTIONS: Questions 21 through 25 are to be answered SOLELY on the basis of the following passage.

    Positive discipline minimizes the amount of personal supervision required and aids in the maintenance of standards. When a new employee has been properly introduced and carefully instructed, when he has come to know the supervisor and has confidence in the supervisor's ability to take care of him, when he willingly cooperates with the supervisor, that employee has been under positive discipline and can be put on his own to produce the quantity and quality of work desired. Negative discipline, the fear of transfer to a less desirable location, for example, to a limited extent may restrain certain individuals from overt violation of rules and regulations governing attendance and conduct which in governmental agencies are usually on at least an agency-wide basis. Negative discipline may prompt employees to perform according to certain rules to avoid a penalty such as, for example, docking for tardiness.

21. According to the above passage, it is reasonable to assume that in the area of discipline, the first-line supervisor in a governmental agency has GREATER scope for action in

    A. *positive* discipline, because negative discipline is largely taken care of by agency rules and regulations
    B. *negative* discipline, because rules and procedures are already fixed and the supervisor can rely on them
    C. *positive* discipline, because the supervisor is in a position to recommend transfers
    D. *negative* discipline, because positive discipline is reserved for people on a higher supervisory level

21.____

22. In order to maintain positive discipline of employees under his supervision, it is MOST important for a supervisor to

    A. assure each employee that he has nothing to worry about
    B. insist at the outset on complete cooperation from employees

22.____

C. be sure that each employee is well trained in his job
D. inform new employees of the penalties for not meeting standards

23. According to the above passage, a feature of negative discipline is that it   23._____

   A. may lower employee morale
   B. may restrain employees from disobeying the rules
   C. censures equal treatment of employees
   D. tends to create standards for quality of work

24. A REASONABLE conclusion based on the above passage is that positive discipline ben-   24._____
efits a supervisor because

   A. he can turn over orientation and supervision of a new employee to one of his sub-
       ordinates
   B. subordinates learn to cooperate with one another when working on an assignment
   C. it is easier to administer
   D. it cuts down, in the long run, on the amount of time the supervisor needs to spend
       on direct supervision

25. Based on the above passage, it is REASONABLE to assume, that an important differ-   25._____
ence between positive discipline and negative discipline is that positive discipline

   A. is concerned with the quality of work and negative discipline with the quantity of
       work
   B. leads to a more desirable basis for motivation of the employee
   C. is more likely to be concerned with agency rules and regulations
   D. uses fear while negative discipline uses penalties to prod employees to adequate
       performance

KEY (CORRECT ANSWERS)

1.	C	11.	B
2.	C	12.	C
3.	D	13.	A
4.	A	14.	A
5.	B	15.	C
6.	D	16.	B
7.	C	17.	C
8.	A	18.	B
9.	D	19.	A
10.	D	20.	B

21.	A
22.	C
23.	B
24.	D
25.	B

TEST 2

DIRECTIONS: Questions 1 through 6 are to be answered SOLELY on the basis of the follow-
                ing passage.

Inherent in all organized endeavors is the need to resolve the individual differences involved in conflict. Conflict may be either a positive or negative factor since it may lead to creativity, innovation and progress on the one hand, or it may result, on the other hand, in a deterioration or even destruction of the organization. Thus, some forms of conflict are desirable, whereas others are undesirable and ethically wrong.

There are three management strategies which deal with interpersonal conflict. In the *divide-and-rule strategy*, management attempts to maintain control by limiting the conflict to those directly involved and preventing their disagreement from spreading to the larger group. The *suppression-of-differences strategy* entails ignoring conflicts or pretending they are irrelevant. In the *working-through-differences strategy*, management actively attempts to solve or resolve intergroup or interpersonal conflicts. Of the three strategies, only the last directly attacks and has the potential for eliminating the causes of conflict. An essential part of this strategy, however, is its employment by a committed and relatively mature management team.

1. According to the above passage, the *divide-and-rule strategy tor* dealing with conflict is   1.____
    the attempt to

    A.   involve other people in the conflict
    B.   restrict the conflict to those participating in it
    C.   divide the conflict into positive and negative factors
    D.   divide the conflict into a number of smaller ones

2. The word *conflict* is used in relation to both positive and negative factors in this passage.   2.____
    Which one of the following words is MOST likely to describe the activity which the word
    conflict, in the sense of the passage, implies?

    A.   Competition   B.   Confusion
    C.   Cooperation   D.   Aggression

3. According to the above passage, which one of the following characteristics is shared by   3.____
    both the *suppression-of-differences strategy* and the *divide-and-rule strategy*?

    A.   Pretending that conflicts are irrelevant
    B.   Preventing conflicts from spreading to the group situation
    C.   Failure to directly attack the causes of conflict
    D.   Actively attempting to resolve interpersonal conflict

4. According to the above passage, the successful resolution of interpersonal conflict   4.____
    requires

    A.   allowing the group to mediate conflicts between two individuals
    B.   division of the conflict into positive and negative factors
    C.   involvement of a committed, mature management team
    D.   ignoring minor conflicts until they threaten the organization

5. Which can be MOST reasonably inferred from the above passage? Conflict between two   5.____
   individuals is LEAST likely to continue when management uses

   A. the *working-through differences strategy*
   B. the *suppression-of differences strategy*
   C. the *divide-and-rule strategy*
   D. a combination of all three strategies

6. According to the above passage, a DESIRABLE result of conflict in an organization is   6.____
   when conflict

   A. exposes production problems in the organization
   B. can be easily ignored by management
   C. results in advancement of more efficient managers
   D. leads to development of new methods

Questions 7-13.

DIRECTIONS: Questions 7 through 13 are to be answered SOLELY on the basis of the passage below.

Modern management places great emphasis on the concept of communication. The
communication process consists of the steps through which an idea or concept passes from
its inception by one person, the sender, until it is acted upon by another person, the receiver.
Through an understanding of these steps and some of the possible barriers that may occur,
more effective communication may be achieved. The first step in the communication process is
ideation by the sender. This is the formation of the intended content of the message he wants
to transmit. In the next step, encoding, the sender organizes his ideas into a series of symbols designed to communicate his message to his intended receiver. He selects suitable
words or phrases that can be understood by the receiver, and he also selects the appropriate
media to be used—for example, memorandum, conference, etc. The third step is transmission
of the encoded message through selected channels in the organizational structure. In the
fourth step, the receiver enters the process by tuning in to receive the message. If the
receiver does not function, however, the message is lost. For example, if the message is oral,
the receiver must be a good listener. The fifth step is decoding of the message by the
receiver, as for example, by changing words into ideas. At this step, the decoded message
may not be the same idea that the sender originally encoded because the sender and
receiver have different perceptions regarding the meaning of certain words. Finally, the
receiver acts or responds. He may file the information, ask for more information, or take other
action. There can be no assurance, however, that communication has taken place unless
there is some type of feedback to the sender in the form of an acknowledgement that the
message was received.

7. According to the above passage, *ideation* is the process by which the   7.____

   A. sender develops the intended content of the message
   B. sender organizes his ideas into a series of symbols
   C. receiver tunes in to receive the message
   D. receiver decodes the message

8. In the last sentence of the passage, the word *feedback* refers to the process by which the sender is assured that the   8.____

    A. receiver filed the information
    B. receiver's perception is the same as his own
    C. message was received
    D. message was properly interpreted

9. Which one of the following BEST shows the order of the steps in the communication process as described in the passage?   9.____

    A. 1 - ideation   2 - encoding
        3 - decoding   4 - transmission
        5 - receiving   6 - action
        7 - feedback to the sender

    B. 1 - ideation   2 - encoding
        3 - transmission   4 - decoding
        5 - receiving   6 - action
        7 - feedback to the sender

    C. 1 - ideation   2 - decoding
        3 - transmission   4 - receiving
        5 - encoding   6 - action
        7 - feedback to the   sender

    D. 1 - ideation   2 - encoding
        3 - transmission   4 - receiving
        5 - decoding   6 - action
        7 - feedback to the sender

10. Which one of the following BEST expresses the main theme of the passage?   10.____

    A. Different individuals have the same perceptions regarding the meaning of words.
    B. An understanding of the steps in the communication process may achieve better communication.
    C. Receivers play a passive role in the communication process.
    D. Senders should not communicate with receivers who transmit feedback.

11. The above passage implies that a receiver does NOT function properly when he   11.____

    A. transmits feedback   B. files the information
    C. is a poor listener   D. asks for more information

12. Which one of the following, according to the above passage, is included in the SECOND step of the communication process?   12.____

    A. Selecting the appropriate media to be used in transmission
    B. Formulation of the intended content of the message
    C. Using appropriate media to respond to the receiver's feedback
    D. Transmitting the message through selected channels in the organization

13. The above passage implies that the *decoding process* is MOST NEARLY the reverse of the _____ process.   13.____

    A. transmission   B. receiving
    C. feedback   D. encoding

Questions 14-19.

DIRECTIONS: Questions 14 through 19 are to be answered SOLELY on the basis of the following passage.

It is often said that no system will work if the people who carry it out do not want it to work. In too many cases, a departmental reorganization that seemed technically sound and economically practical has proved to be a failure because the planners neglected to take the human factor into account. The truth is that employees are likely to feel threatened when they learn that a major change is in the wind. It does not matter whether or not the change actually poses a threat to an employee; the fact that he believes it does or fears it might is enough to make him feel insecure. Among the dangers he fears, the foremost is the possibility that his job may cease to exist and that he may be laid off or shunted into a less skilled position at lower pay. Even if he knows that his own job category is secure, however, he is likely to fear losing some of the important intangible advantages of his present position—for instance, he may fear that he will be separated from his present companions and thrust in with a group of strangers, or that he will find himself in a lower position on the organizational ladder if a new position is created above his.

It is important that management recognize these natural fears and take them into account in planning any kind of major change. While there is no cut-and-dried formula for preventing employee resistance, there are several steps that can be taken to reduce employees' fears and gain their cooperation. First, unwarranted fears can be dispelled if employees are kept informed of the planning from the start and if they know exactly what to expect. Next, assurance on matters such as retraining, transfers, and placement help should be given as soon as it is clear what direction the reorganization will take. Finally, employees' participation in the planning should be actively sought. There is a great psychological difference between feeling that a change is being forced upon one from the outside, and feeling that one is an insider who is helping to bring about a change.

14.   According to the above passage, employees who are not in real danger of losing their jobs because of a proposed reorganization

    A.   will be eager to assist in the reorganization
    B.   will pay little attention to the reorganization
    C.   should not be taken into account in planning the reorganization
    D.   are nonetheless likely to feel threatened by the reorganization

14._____

15.   The passage mentions the *intangible advantages* of a position.
Which of the following BEST describes the kind of advantages alluded to in the passage?

    A.   Benefits such as paid holidays and vacations
    B.   Satisfaction of human needs for things like friendship and status
    C.   Qualities such as leadership and responsibility
    D.   A work environment that meets satisfactory standards of health and safety

15._____

16.   According to the passage, an employee's fear that a reorganization may separate him from his present companions is a (n)

    A.   childish and immature reaction to change
    B.   unrealistic feeling since this is not going to happen

16._____

C. possible reaction that the planners should be aware of
D. incentive to employees to participate in the planning

17. On the basis of the above passage, it would be DESIRABLE, when planning a department-
mental reorganization, to

A. be governed by employee feelings and attitudes
B. give some employees lower positions
C. keep employees informed
D. lay off those who are less skilled

17._____

18. What does the passage say can be done to help gain employees' cooperation in a reorganization?

18._____

A. Making sure that the change is technically sound, that it is economically practical,
and that the human factor is taken into account
B. Keeping employees fully informed, offering help in fitting them into new positions,
and seeking their participation in the planning
C. Assuring employees that they will not be laid off, that they will not be reassigned to
a group of strangers, and that no new positions will be created on the organization
ladder
D. Reducing employees' fears, arranging a retraining program, and providing for
transfers

19. Which of the following suggested titles would be MOST appropriate for this passage?

19._____

A. PLANNING A DEPARTMENTAL REORGANIZATION
B. WHY EMPLOYEES ARE AFRAID
C. LOOKING AHEAD TO THE FUTURE
D. PLANNING FOR CHANGE: THE HUMAN FACTOR

Questions 20-22.

DIRECTIONS: Questions 20 through 22 are to be answered SOLELY on the basis of the following passage.

The achievement of good human relations is essential if a business office is to produce
at top efficiency and is to be a pleasant place in which to work. All office workers plan an
important role in handling problems in human relations. They should, therefore, strive to
acquire the understanding, tactfulness, and awareness necessary to deal effectively with
actual office situations involving co-workers on all levels. Only in this way can they truly
become responsible, interested, cooperative, and helpful members of the staff.

20. The selection implies that the MOST important value of good human relations in an office
is to develop

20._____

A. efficiency
C. tact
B. cooperativeness
D. pleasantness and efficiency

21. Office workers should acquire understanding in dealing with

21._____

A. co-workers
C. superiors
B. subordinates
D. all members of the staff

22. The selection indicates that a highly competent secretary who is also very argumentative   22.____
is meeting office requirements

    A. wholly   B. partly
    C. slightly   D. not at all

Questions 23-25.

DIRECTIONS: Questions 23 through 25 are to be answered SOLELY on the basis of the following passage.

It is common knowledge that ability to do a particular job and performance on the job do
not always go hand in hand. Persons with great potential abilities sometimes fall down on the
job because of laziness or lack of interest in the job, while persons with mediocre talents have
often achieved excellent results through their industry and their loyalty to the interests of their
employers. It is clear; therefore, that in a balanced personnel program, measures of
employee ability need to be supplemented by measures of employee performance, for the
final test of any employee is his performance on the job.

23. The MOST accurate of the following statements, on the basis of the above paragraph, is   23.____
that

    A. employees who lack ability are usually not industrious
    B. an employee's attitudes are more important than his abilities
    C. mediocre employees who are interested in their work are preferable to employees
       who possess great ability
    D. superior capacity for performance should be supplemented with proper attitudes

24. On the basis of the above paragraph, the employee of most value to his employer is NOT   24.____
necessarily the one who

    A. best understands the significance of his duties
    B. achieves excellent results
    C. possesses the greatest talents
    D. produces the greatest amount of work

25. According to the above paragraph, an employee's efficiency is BEST determined by an   25.____

    A. appraisal of his interest in his work
    B. evaluation of the work performed by him
    C. appraisal of his loyalty to his employer
    D. evaluation of his potential ability to perform his work

KEY (CORRECT ANSWERS)

1.	B		11.	C
2.	A		12.	A
3.	C		13.	D
4.	C		14.	D
5.	A		15.	B
6.	D		16.	C
7.	A		17.	C
8.	C		18.	B
9.	D		19.	D
10.	B		20.	D

21.	D
22.	B
23.	D
24.	C
25.	B

———

TEST 3

Questions 1-8.

DIRECTIONS: Questions 1 through 8 are to be answered SOLELY on the basis of the following information and directions.

Assume that you are a clerk in a city agency. Your supervisor has asked you to classify each of the accidents that happened to employees in the agency into the following five categories:

A.   An accident that occurred in the period from January through June, between 9 A.M. and 12 Noon, that was the result of carelessness on the part of the injured employee, that caused the employee to lose less than seven working hours, that happened to an employee who was 40 years of age or over, and who was employed in the agency for less than three years;

B.   An accident that occurred in the period from July through December, after 1 P.M., that was the result of unsafe conditions, that caused the injured employee to lose less than seven working hours, that happened to an employee who was 40 years of age or over, and who was employed in the agency for three years or more;

C.   An accident that occurred in the period from January through June, after 1 P.M., that was the result of carelessness on the part of the injured employee, that caused the injured employee to lose seven or more working hours, that happened to an employee who was less than 40 years old, and who was employed in the agency for three years or more;

D.   An accident that occurred in the period from July through December, between 9 A.M. and 12 Noon, that was the result of unsafe conditions, that caused the injured employee to lose seven or more working hours, that happened to an employee who was less than 40 years old, and who was employed in the agency for less than three years;

E.   Accidents that cannot be classified in any of the foregoing groups. NOTE: In classifying these accidents, an employee's age and length of service are computed as of the date of accident. In all cases, it is to be assumed that each employee has been employed continuously in city service, and that each employee works seven hours a day, from 9 A.M. to 5 P.M., with lunch from 12 Noon to 1 P.M. In each question, consider only the information which will assist you in classifying the accident. Any information which is of no assistance in classifying an accident should not be considered.

1.   The unsafe condition of the stairs in the building caused Miss Perkins to have an accident on October 14, 2003 at 4 P.M. When she returned to work the following day at 1 P.M., Miss Perkins said that the accident was the first one that had occurred to her in her ten years of employment with the agency. She was born on April 27, 1962.

1.____

2.   On the day after she completed her six-month probationary period of employment with the agency, Miss Green, who had been considered a careful worker by her supervisor, injured her left foot in an accident caused by her own carelessness. She went home immediately after the accident, which occurred at 10 A.M., March 19, 2004, but returned to work at the regular time on the following morning. Miss Green was born July 12, 1963 in New York City.

2.____

3.	The unsafe condition of a duplicating machine caused Mr. Martin to injure himself in an accident on September 8, 2006 at 2 P.M. As a result of the accident, he was unable to work the remainder of the day, but returned to his office ready for work on the following morning. Mr. Martin, who has been working for the agency since April 1, 2003, was born in St. Louis on February 1, 1968.		3.____

4.	Mr. Smith was hospitalized for two weeks because of a back injury resulted from an accident on the morning of November 16, 2006. Investigation of the accident revealed that it was caused by the unsafe condition of the floor on which Mr. Smith had been walking. Mr. Smith, who is an accountant, has been anemployee of the agency since March 1, 2004, and was born in Ohio on June 10, 1968.		4.____

5.	Mr. Allen cut his right hand because he was careless in operating a multilith machine. Mr. Allen, who was 33 years old when the accident took place, has been employed by the agency since August 17, 1992. The accident, which occurred on January 26, 2006, at 2 P.M., caused Mr. Allen to be absent from work for the rest of the day. He was able to return to work the next morning.		5.____

6.	Mr. Rand, who is a college graduate, was born on December, 28, 1967, and has been working for the agency since January 7, 2002. On Monday, April 25, 2005, at 2 P.M., his carelessness in operating a duplicating machine caused him to have an accident and to be sent home from work immediately. Fortunately, he was able to return to work at his regular time on the following Wednesday.		6.____

7.	Because he was careless in running down a flight of stairs, Mr. Brown fell, bruising his right hand. Although the accident occurred shortly after he arrived for work on the morning of May 22, 2006, he was unable to resume work until 3 P.M. that day. Mr. Brown was born on August 15, 1955, and began working for the agency on September 12, 2003, as a clerk, at a salary of $22,750 per annum.		7.____

8.	On December 5, 2005, four weeks after he had begun working for the agency, the unsafe condition of an automatic stapling machine caused Mr. Thomas to injure himself in an accident. Mr. Thomas, who was born on May 19,1975, lost three working days because of the accident, which occurred at 11:45 A.M.		8.____

Questions 9-10.

DIRECTIONS:	Questions 9 and 10 are to be answered SOLELY on the basis of the following paragraph.

An impending reorganization within an agency will mean loss by transfer of several professional staff members from the personnel division. The division chief is asked to designate the persons to be transferred. After reviewing the implications of this reduction of staff with his assistant, the division chief discusses the matter at a staff meeting. He adopts the recommendations of several staff members to have volunteers make up the required reduction.

9. The decision to permit personnel to volunteer for transfer is

    A. *poor,* it is not likely that the members of a division are of equal value to the division chief
    B. *good;* dissatisfied members will probably be more productive elsewhere
    C. *poor;* the division chief has abdicated his responsibility to carry out the order given to him
    D. *good;* morale among remaining staff is likely to improve in a more cohesive frame-work

9._____

10. Suppose that one of the volunteers is a recently appointed employee who has completed his probationary period acceptably, but whose attitude toward division operations and agency administration tends to be rather negative and sometimes even abrasive. Because of his lack of commitment to the division, his transfer is recommended. If the transfer is approved, the division chief should, prior to the transfer,

    A. discuss with the staff the importance of commitment to the work of the agency and its relationship with job satisfaction
    B. refrain from any discussion of attitude with the employee
    C. discuss with the employee his concern about the employee's attitude
    D. avoid mention of attitude in the evaluation appraisal prepared for the receiving division chief

10._____

Questions 11-16.

DIRECTIONS: Questions 11 through 16 are to be answered SOLELY on the basis of the following paragraph.

   Methods of administration of office activities, much of which consists of providing information and *know-how* needed to coordinate both activities within that particular office and other offices, have been among the last to come under the spotlight of management analysis. Progress has been rapid during the past decade, however, and is now accelerating at such a pace that an *information revolution* in office management appears to be in the making. Although triggered by technological breakthroughs in electronic computers and other giant steps in mechanization, this information revolution must be attributed to underlying forces, such as the increased complexity of both governmental and private enterprise, and ever-keener competition. Size, diversification, specialization of function, and decentralization are among the forces which make coordination of activities both more imperative and more difficult. Increased competition, both domestic and international, leaves little margin for error in managerial decisions. Several developments during recent years indicate an evolving pattern. In 1960, the American Management Association expanded the scope of its activities and changed the name of its Office Management Division to Administrative Services Division. Also in 1960, the magazine *Office Management* merged with the magazine *American Business*, and this new publication was named *Administrative Management*.

11. A REASONABLE inference that can be made from the information in the above paragraph is that an important role of the office manager today is to

    A. work toward specialization of functions performed by his subordinates
    B. inform and train subordinates regarding any new developments in computer technology and mechanization
    C. assist the professional management analysts with the management analysis work in the organization
    D. supply information that can be used to help coordinate and manage the other activities of the organization

11.____

12. An IMPORTANT reason for the *information revolution* that has been taking place in office management is the

    A. advance made in management analysis in the past decade
    B. technological breakthrough in electronic computers and mechanization
    C. more competitive and complicated nature of private business and government
    D. increased efficiency of office management techniques in the past ten years

12.____

13. According to the above paragraph, specialization of function in an organization is MOST likely to result in

    A. the elimination of errors in managerial decisions
    B. greater need to coordinate activities
    C. more competition with other organizations, both domestic and international
    D. a need for office managers with greater flexibility

13.____

14. The word *evolving,* as used in the third from last sentence in the above paragraph, means MOST NEARLY

    A. developing by gradual changes
    B. passing on to others
    C. occurring periodically
    D. breaking up into separate, constituent parts

14.____

15. Of the following, the MOST reasonable implication of the changes in names mentioned in the last part of the above paragraph is that these groups are attempting to

    A. professionalize the field of office management and the title of Office Manager
    B. combine two publications into one because of the increased costs of labor and materials
    C. adjust to the fact that the field of office management is broadening
    D. appeal to the top managerial people rather than the office management people in business and government

15.____

16. According to the above paragraph, intense competition among domestic and international enterprises makes it MOST important for an organization's managerial staff to

    A. coordinate and administer office activities with other activities in the organization
    B. make as few errors in decision-making as possible
    C. concentrate on decentralization and reduction of size of the individual divisions of the organization
    D. restrict decision-making only to top management officials

16.____

Questions 17-21.

DIRECTIONS: Questions 17 through 21 are to be answered SOLELY on the basis of the following passage.

For some office workers, it is useful to be familiar with the four main classes of domestic mail; for others, it is essential. Each class has a different rate of postage, and some have requirements concerning wrapping, sealing, or special information to be placed on the package. First class mail, the class which may not be opened for postal inspection, includes letters, postcards, business reply cards, and other kinds of written matter. There are different rates for some of the kinds of cards which can be sent by first class mail. The maximum weight for an item sent by first class mail is 70 pounds. An item which is not letter size should be marked *First Class* on all sides. Although office workers most often come into contact with first class mail, they may find it helpful to know something about the other classes. Second class mail is generally used for mailing newspapers and magazines. Publishers of these articles must meet certain U.S. Postal Service requirements in order to obtain a permit to use second class mailing rates. Third class mail, which must weigh less than 1 pound, includes printed materials and merchandise parcels. There are two rate structures for this class - a single piece rate and a bulk rate. Fourth class mail, also known as parcel post, includes packages weighing from one to 40 pounds. For more information about these classes of mail and the actual mailing rates, contact your local post office.

17. According to this passage, first class mail is the *only* class which   17.____

    A. has a limit on the maximum weight of an item
    B. has different rates for items within the class
    C. may not be opened for postal inspection
    D. should be used by office workers

18. According to this passage, the one of the following items which may CORRECTLY be   18.____
sent by fourth class mail is a

    A. magazine weighing one-half pound
    B. package weighing one-half pound
    C. package weighing two pounds
    D. postcard

19. According to this passage, there are different postage rates for   19.____

    A. a newspaper sent by second class mail and a magazine sent by second class mail
    B. each of the classes of mail
    C. each pound of fourth class mail
    D. printed material sent by third class mail and merchandise parcels sent by third class mail

20. In order to send a newspaper by second class mail, a publisher MUST   20.____

    A. have met certain postal requirements and obtained a permit
    B. indicate whether he wants to use the single piece or the bulk rate
    C. make certain that the newspaper weighs less than one pound
    D. mark the newspaper *Second Class* on the top and bottom of the wrapper

21. Of the following types of information, the one which is NOT mentioned in the passage is   21.____
    the

    A. class of mail to which parcel post belongs
    B. kinds of items which can be sent by each class of mail
    C. maximum weight for an item sent by fourth class mail
    D. postage rate for each of the four classes of mail

Questions 22-25.

DIRECTIONS: Questions 22 through 25 are to be answered SOLELY on the basis of the fol-
             lowing paragraph.

A standard comprises characteristics attached to an aspect of a process or product by
which it can be evaluated. Standardization is the development and adoption of standards.
When they are formulated, standards are not usually the product of a single person, but represent the thoughts and ideas of a group, leavened with the knowledge and information which
are currently available. Standards which do not meet certain basic requirements become a
hindrance rather than an aid to progress. Standards must not only be correct, accurate, and
precise in requiring no more and no less than what is needed for satisfactory results, but they
must also be workable in the sense that their usefulness is not nullified by external conditions.
Standards should also be acceptable to the people who use them. If they are not acceptable,
they cannot be considered to be satisfactory, although they may possess all the other essential characteristics.

22. According to the above paragraph, a processing standard that requires the use of mate-   22.____
    rials that cannot be procured is MOST likely to be

    A. incomplete   B. unworkable
    C. inaccurate   D. unacceptable

23. According to the above paragraph, the construction of standards to which the perfor-   23.____
    mance of job duties should conform is MOST often

    A. the work of the people responsible for seeing that the duties are properly per-
       formed
    B. accomplished by the person who is best informed about the functions involved
    C. the responsibility of the people who are to apply them
    D. attributable to the efforts of various informed persons

24. According to the above paragraph, when standards call for finer tolerances than those   24.____
    essential to the conduct of successful production operations, the effect of the standards
    on the improvement of production operations is

    A. negative   B. negligible
    C. nullified   D. beneficial

25. The one of the following which is the MOST suitable title for the above paragraph is   25.____

    A. THE EVALUATION OF FORMULATED STANDARDS
    B. THE ATTRIBUTES OF SATISFACTORY STANDARDS
    C. THE ADOPTION OF ACCEPTABLE STANDARDS
    D. THE USE OF PROCESS OR PRODUCT STANDARDS

KEY (CORRECT ANSWERS)

1.	B		11.	D
2.	A		12.	C
3.	E		13.	B
4.	D		14.	A
5.	E		15.	C
6.	C		16.	B
7.	A		17.	C
8.	D		18.	C
9.	A		19.	B
10.	C		20.	A

21.	D
22.	C
23.	D
24.	A
25.	B

ARITHMETICAL REASONING
EXAMINATION SECTION
TEST 1

DIRECTIONS: Each question or incomplete statement is followed by several suggested answers or completions. Select the one that BEST answers the question or completes the statement. *PRINT THE LETTER OF THE CORRECT ANSWER IN THE SPACE AT THE RIGHT.*

1. In 2015, a public agency spent $180 to buy pencils that cost three cents each. In 2017, the agency spent $420 to buy the same number of pencils that it had bought in 2015. The price per pencil that the agency paid in 2017 was _____ cents.

   A. 6 1/3   B. 2/3   C. 7   D. 7 3/4   1._____

2. A stenographer spent her 35 hour work week on taking dictation, transcribing the dictated material, and filing.
   If she spent 20% of the work week on taking dictation and 1/2 of the remaining time on transcribing the dictated material, the number of hours of the work week that she spent on filing was

   A. 7   B. 10.5   C. 14   D. 17.5   2._____

3. A typist typed eight pages in two hours.
   If she typed an average of 50 lines per page and an average of 12 words per line, what was her typing speed, in words per minute?

   A. 40   B. 50   C. 60   D. 80   3._____

4. The daily compensation to be paid to each consultant hired in a certain agency is computed by dividing his professional earnings in the previous year by 250. The maximum daily compensation they can receive is $200 each. Four consultants who were hired to work on a special project had the following professional earnings in the previous year: $37,500, $144,000, $46,500, and $61,100. What will be the TOTAL daily cost to the agency for these four consultants?

   A. $932   B. $824   C. $736   D. $712   4._____

5. In a typing and stenographic pool consisting of 30 employees, 2/5 of them are typists, 1/3 of them are senior typists and senior stenographers, and the rest are stenographers. If there are 5 more stenographers than senior stenographers, how many senior stenographers are in the typing and stenographic pool?

   A. 3   B. 5   C. 8   D. 10   5._____

6. There are 3,330 copies of a three-page report to be collated. One clerk starts collating at 9:00 A.M. and is joined 15 minutes later by two other clerks. It takes 15 minutes for each of these clerks to collate 90 copies of the report.
   At what time should the job be completed if all three clerks continue working at the same rate without breaks?

   A. 12:00 Noon   B. 12:15 P.M.   6._____
   C. 1:00 P.M.   D. 1:15 P.M.

7. By the end of last year, membership in the blood credit program in a certain agency had increased from the year before by 500, bringing the total to 2,500.
If the membership increased by the same percentage this year, the TOTAL number of members in the blood credit program for this agency by the end of this year should be

   A. 2,625   B. 3,000   C. 3,125   D. 3,250

8. During this year, an agency suggestion program put into practice suggestions from 24 employees, thereby saving the agency 40 times the amount of money it paid in awards. If 1/3 of the employees were awarded $50 each, 1/2 of the employees were awarded $25 each, and the rest were awarded $10 each, how much money did the agency save by using the suggestions?

   A. $18,760   B. $29,600   C. C, $32,400   D. $46,740

9. A senior stenographer earned $20,100 a year and had 4.5% state tax withheld for the year.
If she was paid every two weeks, the amount of state tax that was taken out of each of her paychecks, based on a 52-week year, was MOST NEARLY

   A. $31.38   B. $32.49   C. $34.77   D. $36.99

10. Two stenographers have been assigned to address 750 envelopes. One stenographer addresses twice as many envelopes per hour as the other stenographer.
If it takes five hours for them to complete the job, the rate of the slower stenographer is _____ envelopes per hour.

   A. 35   B. 50   C. 75   D. 100

11. Suppose that the postage rate for mailing single copies of a magazine to persons not included on a subscription list is 18 cents for the first two ounces of the single copy and 3 cents for each additional ounce.
If 19 copies of a magazine, each of which weighs eleven ounces, are mailed to 19 different people, the TOTAL postage cost of these magazines is

   A. $3.42   B. $3.99   C. $6.18   D. $8.55

12. A senior stenographer spends about 40 hours a month taking dictation. Of that time, 44% is spent taking minutes of meetings, 38% is spent taking dictation of lengthy reports, and the rest of the time is spent taking dictation of letters and memoranda.
How much MORE time is spent taking minutes of meetingsthan in taking dictation of letters and memoranda?
10 hours _____ minutes.

   A. 6   B. 16   C. 24   D. 40

13. In one week, a stenographer typed 65 letters. Forty letters had 4 copies on colored paper. The rest had 3 copies on colored paper.
If the stenographer had 500 sheets of colored paper on hand at the beginning of the week when she started typing the letters, how many sheets of colored paper did she have left at the end of the week?

   A. 190   B. 235   C. 265   D. 305

14. An agency is planning to microfilm letters and other correspondence of the last five years. The number of letter-size documents that can be photographed on a 100-foot roll of microfilm is 2,995. The agency estimates that it will need 240 feet of microfilm to do all the pages of all of the letters.
How many pages of letter-size documents can be photographed on this microfilm?

    A. 5,990   B. 6,786   C. 7,188   D. 7,985

14._____

15. In an agency, 2/3 of the total number of female stenographers and 1/2 of the total number of male stenographers attended a general staff meeting.
If there are a total of 56 stenographers in the agency and 25% of them are male, the number of female stenographers who attended the general staff meeting is

    A. 14   B. 28   C. 36   D. 42

15._____

16. A worker is currently earning $17,140 a year and pays $350 a month for rent. He expects to get a raise that will enable him to move into an apartment where his rent will be 25% of his new yearly salary.
If this new apartment is going to cost him $390 a month, what is the TOTAL amount of raise that he expects to get?

    A. $480   B. $980   C. $1,580   D. $1,840

16._____

17. The tops of five desks in an office are to be covered with a scratch-resistant material. Each desk top measures 60 inches by 36 inches.
How many square feet of material will be needed for the five desk tops?

    A. 15   B. 75   C. 96   D. 180

17._____

18. Three grades of bond paper are used in a central transcribing unit. The cost per ream of paper is $1.90 for Grade A, $1.70 for Grade B, and $1.60 for Grade C.
If the central transcribing unit used 6 reams of Grade A paper, 14 reams of Grade B paper, and 20 reams of Grade C paper, the AVERAGE cost, per ream, of the bond paper used by this unit is between

    A. $1.62 and $1.66   B. $1.66 and $1.70
    C. $1.70 and $1.74   D. $1.74 and $1.80

18._____

19. The Complaint Bureau of a city agency is composed of an investigation unit, a clerical unit, and a central transcribing unit. The sum of $264,000 has been appropriated for the operation of this bureau. Of this sum, $170,000 is to be allotted to the clerical unit.
Of this bureau's total appropriation, the percentage that is left for the central transcribing unit is MOST NEARLY _____ if $41,200 is allotted for investigations.

    A. 20%   B. 30%   C. 40%   D. 50%

19._____

20. Three typists were assigned to address a total of 2,655 postcards. Typist A addressed the postcards at the rate of 170 per hour. Typist B addressed the postcards at the rate of 150 per hour. Typist C's rate is not known. After the three typists had addressed postcards for three and a half hours, Typist C was taken off this assignment. It was necessary for Typist A and Typist B to work two and a half hours more to complete this assignment. The rate per hour at which Typist C addressed the postcards was

20._____

A. less than 150
B. between 150 and 170
C. more than 170 but less than 200
D. more than 200

21. In 2015, a city agency bought 12,000 envelopes at $4.00 per hundred. In 2016, the price of envelopes purchased was 40 percent higher than the 2010 price, but only 60 percent as many envelopes were bought.
The total cost of the envelopes purchased in 2016 was MOST NEARLY

    A. $250   B. $320   C. $400   D. $480

21.____

22. A stenographer has been assigned to place entries on 500 forms. She places entries on 25 forms by the end of half an hour, when she is joined by another stenographer. The second stenographer places entries at the rate of 45 an hour.
Assuming that both stenographers continue to work at their respective rates of speed, the TOTAL number of hours required to carry out the entire assignment is

    A. 5   B. 54   C. 64   D. 7

22.____

23. On Monday, a stenographer took dictation without interruption for 1 1/2 hours and transcribed all the dictated material in 3 1/2 hours. On Tuesday, she took dictation uninterruptedly for 1 3/4 hours and transcribed all the material in 3 3/4 hours. On Wednesday, she took dictation without interruption for 2 1/4 hours and transcribed all the material in 4 1/2 hours.
If she took dictation at the average rate of 90 words per minute during these three days, then her average transcription rate, in words per minute, for the same three days was MOST NEARLY

    A. 36   B. 41   C. 54   D. 58

23.____

24. In a division of clerks and stenographers, 15 people are currently employed, 20% of whom are stenographers.
If management plans are to maintain the current number of stenographers, but to increase the clerical staff to the point where 12% of the total staff are stenographers, what is the MAXIMUM number of additional clerks that should be hired to meet these plans?

    A. 3   B. 8   C. 10   D. 12

24.____

25. In the first quarter of the year, a certain operator sent out 230 quarterly reports. In the second quarter of that year, he sent out 310 quarterly reports.
The percent increase in the number of quarterly reports he sent out in the second quarter of the year compared to the first quarter of the year is MOST NEARLY

    A. 26%   B. 29%   C. 35%   D. 39%

25.____

KEY (CORRECT ANSWERS)

1.	C	11.	D
2.	C	12.	C
3.	A	13.	C
4.	C	14.	C
5.	A	15.	B
6.	B	16.	C
7.	C	17.	B
8.	B	18.	B
9.	C	19.	A
10.	B	20.	D

21.	C
22.	B
23.	B
24.	C
25.	C

SOLUTIONS TO PROBLEMS

1. $180 ÷ .03 = 6000 pencils bought. In 2017, the price per pencil = $420 / 6000 = .07 = 7 cents.

2. Number of hours on filing = 35 - (.20)(35) - (1/2)(28) = 14

3. Eight pages contains (8)(50)(12) = 4800 words. She thus typed 4800 words in 120 minutes = 40 words per minute.

4. $37,500 ÷ 250 = $150; $144,000 ÷ 250 = $576; $46,500 ÷ 250 = $186; $61,100 ÷ 250 = $244.40 Since $200 = maximum compensation for any single consultant, total compensation = $150 + $200 + $186 + $200 = $736

5. Number of typists = (2/5)(30) = 12, number of senior typists and senior stenographers = (1/3)(30) = 10, number of stenographers = 30 - 12 - 10 = 8. Finally, number of senior stenographers = 8-5 = 3

6. At 9:15 AM, 90 copies have been collated. The remaining 3240 copies are being collated at the rate of (3)(90) = 270 every 15 minutes = 1080 per hour. Since 3240 ÷ 1080 = 3 hours, the clerks will finish at 9:15 AM + 3 hours = 12:15 PM.

7. During last year, the membership increased from 2000 to 2500, which represents a (500/2000)(100) = 25% increase. A 25% increase during this year means the membership = (2500)(1.25) = 3125

8. Total awards = (1/3)(24)($50) + (1/2)(24)($25) + (1/6)(24)($10) = $740. Thus, the savings = (40)($740) = $29,600

9. Her pay for 2 weeks = $20,100 ÷ 26 ≈ $773.08. Thus, her state tax for 2 weeks ≈ ($773.08)(.045) ≈ $34.79. (Nearest correct answer is $34.77 in four selections.)

10. 750 ÷ 5 hours = 150 envelopes per hour for the 2 stenographers combined. Let x = number of envelopes addressed by the slower stenographer . Then, x + 2x = 150. Solving, x = 50

11. Total cost = (19)[.18+(.03)(9)] = $8.55

12. (.44)(40) - (.18)(40) = 10.4 hrs. = 10 hrs. 24 rain.

13. 500 - (40)(4) - (25)(3) = 265

14. 2995 ÷ 100 = 29.95 documents per foot of microfilm roll. Then, (29.95)(240 ft) = 7188 documents

15. There are (.75)(56) = 42 female stenographers. Then, (2/3)(42) = 28 of them attended the meeting.

16. ($390)(12) = $4680 new rent per year. Then, ($4680)(4) = $18,720 = his new yearly salary. His raise = $18,720 - $17,140 = $1580

17. Number of sq.ft. = (5)(60)(36) ÷ 144 = 75

18. Average cost per ream = [($1.90)(6) + ($1.70) (14) + ($1.60) (20)] / 40 = $1.68, which is between $1.66 and $1.70

19. $264,000 - $170,000 - $41,200 = 52,800 = 20%

20. Let x = typist C's rate. Since typists A and B each worked 6 hrs., while typist C worked only 3.5 hrs., we have (6)(170) + (6)(150) + 3.5x = 2655. Solving, x = 210, which is nore than 200.

21. In 2016, the cost per hundred envelopes was ($4.00)(1.40) = $5.60 and (.60)(12,000) = 7200 envelopes were bought. Total cost in 2016 = (72)($5.60) = $403.20, or about $400.

22. The 1st stenographer's rate is 50 forms per hour. After 1/2 hr., there are 500 - 25 = 475 forms to be done and the combined rate of the 2 stenographers is 95 forms per hr. Thus, total hrs. required = 1/2 + (475) ÷ (95) = 5 1/2

23. Total time for dictation = 1 1/4 + 1 3/4 + 2 1/4 = 5 1/4 hrs. = 315 min. The number of words = (90)(315) = 28,350. The total transcription 3 time = 3 1/4 + 3 3/4 + 44 = 11 1/2 hrs. = 690 min. Her average transcription rate

= 28,350 ÷ 690 ≈ 41 words per min.

24. Currently, there are (.20)(15) = 3 stenographers, and thus 12 clerks. Let x = additional clerks. Then, $\frac{3}{3+12+x} = .12$. This simplifies to 3 = (.12)(15+x). Solving, x = 10

25. Percent increase = $(\frac{80}{230})(100) \approx 35\%$

TEST 2

DIRECTIONS: Each question or incomplete statement is followed by several suggested answers or completions. Select the one that BEST answers the question or completes the statement. *PRINT THE LETTER OF THE CORRECT ANSWER IN THE SPACE AT THE RIGHT.*

1. A school has 112 homeroom classes. There were 15 school days in February. The aggregate register of the school for the month of February was 52,920; the aggregate attendance was 43,860.
   The average class size, to the NEAREST tenth, is

   1.____

   A. 35.3   B. 31.5   C. 29.2   D. 26.9

2. As the school secretary in charge of supplies, you are asked to order the following items on a supplementary requisition for general supplies:
   5 gross of red pencils at $8.90 per dozen
   5,000 manila envelopes at $2.35 per C
   36 rulers at $187.20 per gross
   6 boxes of manila paper at $307.20 per carton (24 boxes to a carton)
   180 reams of composition paper at $27.80 per carton (20 reams to a carton)
   The TOTAL amount of the order is

   2.____

   A. $957.20   B. $1,025.30   C. $916.80   D. $991.30

3. In the high school to which you have been assigned as a school secretary, the annual allotment for general supplies, textbooks, repairs, etc. for the school year 2015-16 was $37,500. A special allotment of $10,000 was granted for textbooks ordered from the State Textbook List. The original requisition for general and vocational supplies amounted to $12,514.75; for science supplies, $6,287.25; for textbooks, including the special funds, $13,785.00; monies spent for equipment repairs and science perishables through December 31, 2015, $1,389.68.
   The balance in your supply allotment account on January 1, 2016 will be

   3.____

   A. $14,913.00   B. $13,523.32
   C. $17,308.32   D. $3,523.32

4. The teacher of one of the sixth term typing classes in the high school to which you are assigned as a school secretary has agreed to have her students type attendance cards for the incoming students for the new school year, commencing in September, as a work project. There are 24 students in the class; each student can complete 8 cards during a typing period. There will be 4,032 new students in September.
   The number of typing periods required to complete the task is

   4.____

   A. 31   B. 21   C. 28   D. 24

5. As a school secretary assigned to payroll duties, you are required to prepare the extra-curricular payroll report for the coaches teams in your high school. The rate of pay for these activities was increased on November 1 from $148 per session to $174.50 per session. The pay period which you are reporting is for the months of October, November, and December. Mr. Jones, the football coach, conducted 15 practice sessions in October, 20 in November, and 30 in December.
   His TOTAL gross pay on the December extra-curricular payroll report is

   5.____

A. $10,547.50
C. $10,945.00
B. $10,415.00
D. $11,342.50

6. The comparative results on a uniform examination given in your school for the last three years follow: 6._____

	2014	2015	2016
Number taking test	501	496	485
Number passing test	441	437	436

The percentage of passing, to the nearest tenth of a percent, for the year in which the HIGHEST percent of students passed is

A. 89.3%   B. 88%   C. 89.9%   D. 90.3%

7. During his first seven terms in high school, a student compiled the following averages: 7._____

Term	Numbers of Majors Completed	Average
1	4	81.25%
2	4	83.75%
3	5	86.2%
4	5	85.8%
5	5	87.0%
6	5	83.4%
7	5	82.6%

In his eighth term, the student had the following final marks in major subjects: 90%, 95%, 80%, 90%, 85%. The student's average for all eight terms of high school, correct to the nearest tenth of a percent, is

A. 84.8%   B. 84.7%   C. 84.9%   D. 85.8%

8. A secretary is asked by her employer to order an office machine which lists at a price of $360, less trade discounts of 20% and 10%, terms 2/10, n/30. There is a delivery charge of $8 and an installation charge of $12. If the machine is paid for in 10 days, the TOTAL cost of the machine will be 8._____

A. $264.80   B. $258.40   C. $266.96   D. $274.02

9. The school to which you have been assigned as school secretary has an annual allowance of 5,120 hours for all teacher aides. The principal decides to employ 5 teacher aides from 8:00 A.M. to 12:00 Noon, and 5 other teacher aides from 12:00 Noon to 4:00 P.M. daily for as many days as his allowance permits. 9._____
If a teacher aide earns $17.00 an hour, and he is present every day, his TOTAL earnings for the school year will be more than

A. $7,000 but less than $8,000
B. $8,000 but less than $9,000
C. $9,000 but less than $10,000
D. $10,000

10. During examination week in a high school to which you have been assigned as school secretary, teachers are required to be in school at least 6 hours and 20 minutes daily although their arrival and departure times may vary each day. A teacher's time card that you have been asked to check shows the following entries for the week of June 17:   10.____

Date	Arrival	Departure
17	7:56 AM	2:18 PM
18	9:53 AM	4:22 PM
19	12:54 PM	7:03 PM
20	9:51 AM	4:15 PM
21	7:58 AM	2:11 PM

During the week of June 17 to June 21, the teacher was in school for AT LEAST the minimum required time on _____ days.

   A. 2 of the 5   B. 3 of the 5
   C. 4 of the 5   D. all 5

11. As school secretary, you are asked to find the total of the following bill received in your school: 11.____

    750 yellow envelopes at $.22 per C
    2,400 white envelopes at $2.80 per M
    30 rulers at $5.04 per gross
The TOTAL of the bill is

   A. $69.90   B. $24.27   C. $18.87   D. $9.42

12. A department in the school to which you have been assigned as school secretary has been given a textbook allowance of $5,500 for the school year. The department's textbook order is: 12.____

    75 books at $32.50 each
    45 books at $49.50 each
    25 books at $34.50 each
The TOTAL of the department's order is _____ the allowance.

   A. $27.50 over   B. $27.50 under
   C. $72.50 under   D. $57.50 over

13. The total receipts, including 5% city sales tax, for the G.O. store for the first week of school amounted to $489.09.
The receipts from the G.O. store for the first week of school, excluding the 5% city sales tax, amounted to   13.____

   A. $465.80   B. $464.64   C. $464.63   D. $513.54

14. Class sizes in the school to which you have been assigned as school secretary are as follows: 14.____

Number of Classes	Class Size
9	29 pupils
12	31 pupils
15	32 pupils
7	33 pupils
11	34 pupils

The average class size in this school, correct to the nearest tenth, is

   A. 30.8   B. 31.9   C. 31.8   D. 30.9

15. In 2013, the social security tax was 4.2% for the first $6,600 earned a year. In 2014, the   15._____
social security tax was 4.4% on the first $6,600 earned a year.
For a teacher aide earning $19,200 in 2013 and $20,400 in 2014, the increase in
social security tax deduction in 2014 over 2013 was

   A. $132.00   B. $13.20   C. $19.20   D. $20.40

16. A teacher aide earning $23,900 a year will incur automatic deductions of 3.90% for social   16._____
security and .50% for medicare, based on the first $6,600 a year earnings. The TOTAL
tax deduction for these two items will be

   A. $274   B. $290.40   C. $525.80   D. $300.40

17. The school store turns in receipts totaling $131.25 to the school treasurer, including 5%   17._____
which has been collected for sales tax.
The amount of money which the treasurer MUST set aside for sales tax is

   A. $6.56   B. $6.25   C. $5.00   D. $5.25

18. One of the custodial assistants can wash all the windows in the main office in 3 hours. A   18._____
second assistant can wash the windows in the main office in 2 hours.
If the two men work together, they should complete the task in _____ hour(s) _____
minutes.

   A.   1; 0   B.   1.5; 0   C.   1; 12   D.   1; 15

19. A school secretary is requested by the principal to order an office machine which lists at   19._____
a price of $120, less discounts of 10% and 5%.
The net price of the machine to the school will be

   A. $100.50   B. $102.00   C. $102.60   D. $103.00

20. Five students are employed at school under a work-study program through which they   20._____
are paid $10.00 an hour for work in school offices, but no student may earn more than
$450 a month. Three days before the end of the month, you note that the student payroll
totals $2,062.50.
The number of hours which each of the students may work during the remainder of the
month is_____hour(s).

   A.   4   B.   2   C.   1   D.   3

21. You are asked to summarize expenditures made by the school within the budget alloca-   21._____
tion for the school year. You determine that the following expenditures have been made:
educational supplies, $2,600; postage, $650; emergency repairs, $225; textbooks,
$5,100; instructional equipment, $1,200.
Since $10,680 has been allocated to the school, the following sum still remains avail-
able for office supplies:

   A. $905   B. $1,005   C. $800   D. $755

22. In preparing the percentage of attendance for the period report, you note that the aggre-   22.____
    gate attendance is 57,585 and the aggregate register is 62,000.
    The percentage of attendance, to the nearest tenth of a percent, is

       A. 91.9%   B. 93.0%   C. 92.8%   D. 92.9%

23. You borrow $1,200 from your retirement fund which you must repay over a period of   23.____
    three years, with interest of $144, each payment to be divided equally among 36 total
    payments.
    The monthly deduction from your paycheck will be

       A. $37.33   B. $36.00   C. $33.00   D. $37.30

24. Tickets for a school dance are printed, starting with number 401 and ending with number   24.____
    1650. They are to be sold for 750 each. The tickets remaining unsold should start with
    number 1569.
    The amount of cash which should be collected for the sale of tickets is

       A. $876.75   B. $937.50   C. $876.00   D. $875.25

25. Stage curtains are purchased by the school and delivered on October 3 under terms of   25.____
    5/10, 2/30, net/60. The curtains are paid in full by a check for $522.50 on October 12.
    The invoice price was

       A. $533.16   B. $522.50   C. $540.00   D. $550.00

KEY (CORRECT ANSWERS)

1.	B		11.	D
2.	B		12.	A
3.	B		13.	A
4.	B		14.	C
5.	C		15.	B
6.	C		16.	B
7.	C		17.	B
8.	D		18.	C
9.	B		19.	C
10.	B		20.	D

21.	A
22.	D
23.	A
24.	C
25.	D

———

SOLUTIONS TO PROBLEMS

1. Average class size = 52,920 ÷ 15 ÷ 112 = 31.5

2. Total amount = (5)(12)($8.90) + (50)($2.35) + (36) ($187.20) ÷ 144 +
   (6)($307.20) ÷ 24 + (9)($27.80) = $1025.30

3. Balance = $37,500 + $10,000 - $12,514.75 - $6287.25 - $13,785 - $1389.68 =
   $13,523.32

4. (24)(8) = 192 cards completed in one period. Then, 4032 ÷ 192 = 21 typing periods
   required.

5. Total pay = (15)($148.00) + (20)($174.50) + (30)($174.50) = $10,945.00

6. The passing rates for 2014, 2015, 2016 were 88.0%, 88.1%, and 89.9%, respectively. So, 89.9% was the highest.

7. His 8th term average was 88.0%. His overall average for all 8 terms =
   [(4)(81.25%)+(4)(83.75%)+(5)(86.2%)+(5)(85.8%)+
   (5)(87.0%)+(5)(83.4%)+(5)(82.6%)+(5)(88.0%)] ÷ 38 = 84.9%

8. Total cost = ($360)(.80)(.90)(.98) + $8 + $12 ≈ $274.02 (Exact amount =
   $274.016)

9. 5120 ÷ 4 = 1280 teacher-days. Then, 1280 ÷ 10 = 128 days per teacher. A
   teacher's earnings for these 128 days = ($17.00)(4)(128)= $8704, which is more
   than $8000 but less than $9000.

10. The number of hours present on each of the 5 days listed was 6 hrs. 22 min., 6 hrs.
    29 min., 6 hrs. 9 min., 6 hrs. 24 min., and 6 hrs. 13 min. On 3 days, he met the minimum time.

11. Total cost = (7.5)(.22) + (2.4)($2.80) + (30/144)(5.04) = $9.42

12. Textbook order = (75)($32.50) + (45)($49.50) + (25)($34.50) = $5527.50, which is
    $27.50 over the allowance.

13. Receipts without the tax = $489.09 ÷ 1.05 = $465.80

14. Average class size = [(9)(29)+(12)(31)+(7)(33)+(11)(34)+(15)(32)] ÷ 54 ≈ 31.8

15. ($6600)(.044-.042) = $13.20

16. ($6600)(.039+.005) = $290.40

17. $131.25 = 1.05x, x = 125, $131.25 - 125.00 = 6.25

18. Let x = hours needed working together. Then, (1/3)(x) + (1/2)(x) = 1
    Simplifying, 2x + 3x = 6. Solving, x = 1 1/5 hrs. = 1 hr. 12 min.

19. Net price = 120 - 10% (12) = 108; 108 - 5% (5.40) = 102.60

20. ($225)(5) - $1031.25 = $93.75 remaining in the month. Since the 5 students earn
    $25 per hour combined, $93.75 ÷ $25 = 3.75, which must be rounded down to 3
    hours.

21. $10,680 - $2600 - $650 - $225 - $5100 - $1200 = $905 for office supplies.

22. 57,585 ÷ 62,000 ≈ .9288 ≈ 92.9%

23. Monthly deduction = $1344 ÷ 36 = $37.33 (Technically, 35 payments of $37.33
    and 1 payment of $37.45)

24. (1569-401)(.75) = $876.00

25. The invoice price (which reflects the 5% discount) is $522.50 ÷ .95 = $550.00

————————————

TEST 3

DIRECTIONS: Each question or incomplete statement is followed by several suggested answers or completions. Select the one that BEST answers the question or completes the statement. *PRINT THE LETTER OF THE CORRECT ANSWER IN THE SPACE AT THE RIGHT.*

1. If an inch on an office layout drawing equals 4 feet of actual floor dimension, then a room which actually measures 9 feet by 14 feet is represented on the drawing by measurements equaling _____ inches x _____ inches.　　1.____

   A. 2 1/4; 3 1/2　　B. 2 1/2; 3 1/2　　C. 2 1/4;3 1/4　　D. 2 1/2;3 1/4

2. A cooperative education intern works from 1:30 P.M. to 5 P.M. on Mondays, Wednesdays, and Fridays, and from 10 A.M. to 2:30 P.M. with no lunch hour on Tuesdays and Thursdays. He earns $13.50 an hour on this job. In addition, he has a Saturday job paying $16.00 an hour at which he works from 9 A.M. to 3 P.M. with a half hour off for lunch. The gross amount that the student earns each week is MOST NEARLY　　2.____

   A. $321.90　　B. $355.62　　C. $364.02　　D. $396.30

3. Thirty-five percent of the College Discovery students who entered community college earned an associate degree. Of these students, 89% entered senior college, of which 67% went on to earn baccalaureate degrees.
   If there were 529 College Discovery students who entered community college, then the number of those who went on to finally receive a baccalaureate degree is MOST NEARLY　　3.____

   A. 354　　B. 315　　C. 124　　D. 110

4. It takes 5 office assistants two days to type 125 letters. Each of the assistants works at an equal rate of speed. How many days will it take 10 office assistants to type 200 letters?　　4.____

   A. 1　　B. 1 3/5　　C. 2　　D. 2 1/5

5. The following are the grades and credits earned by Student X during the first two years in college.　　5.____

Grade	Credits	Weight	Quality Points
A	10 1/2	x4	
B	24	x3	
C	12	x2	
D	4 1/2	x1	
F, FW	5	x0	

   To compute an index number:
   - I. Multiply the number of credits of each grade by the weight to get the number of *quality points.*
   - II. Add the credits.
   - III. Add the quality points.
   - IV. Divide the total quality points by the total credits, and carry the division to two decimal places.

   On the basis of the given information, the index number for Student X is

   A. 2.54　　B. 2.59　　C. 2.63　　D. 2.68

6. Typist X can type 20 forms per hour, and Typist Y can type 30 forms per hour. If there are 30 forms to be typed and both typists are put to work on the job, how soon should they be expected to finish the work?
   _____ minutes.

   A. 32   B. 34   C. 36   D. 38

   6._____

7. Assume that there were 18 working days in February and that the six clerks in your unit had the following number of absences:

Clerk	Absences
F	3
G	2
H	8
I	1
J	0
K	5

   The average percentage attendance for the six clerks in your unit in February was MOST NEARLY

   A. 80%   B. 82%   C. 84%   D. 86%

   7._____

8. A certain employee is paid at the rate of $7.50 per hour, with time and a half for overtime. Hours in excess of 40 hours a week count as overtime. During the past week, the employee put in 48 working hours. The employee's gross wages for the week are MOST NEARLY

   A. $330   B. $350   C. $370   D. $390

   8._____

9. You are making a report on the number of inside and outside calls handled by a particular switchboard. Over a 15-day period, the total number of all inside and outside calls handled by the switchboard was 5,760. The average number of inside calls per day was 234. You cannot find one day's tally of outside calls, but the total number of outside calls for the other fourteen days was 2,065. From this information, how many outside calls must have been reported on the missing tally?

   A. 175   B. 185   C. 195   D. 205

   9._____

10. A floor plan has been prepared for a new building, drawn to a scale of 3/4 inch = 1 foot. A certain area is drawn 1 and 1/2 feet long and 6 inches wide on the floor plan. What are the ACTUAL dimensions of this area in the new building?
    _____ feet long and _____ feet wide.

    A. 21; 8   B. 24; 8   C. 27; 9   D. 30; 9

    10._____

11. You are preparing a package of six books to mail to a professor who is on sabbatical. They weigh, respectively, 1 pound 11 ounces, 1 pound 6 ounces, 2 pounds 1 ounce, 2 pounds 2 ounces, 1 pound 7 ounces, and 1 pound 8 ounces. The packaging material weighs 6 ounces.
    The TOTAL weight of the package will be_____ pounds _____ ounces.

    A. 10; 3   B. 10; 9   C. 11; 5   D. 12; 5

    11._____

12. Part-time students are charged $70 per credit for courses at a particular college. In addition, they must pay a $24.00 student activity fee if they take six credits or more and $14.00 lab fee for each laboratory course.
If a person takes one 3-credit course and one 4-credit course and his 4-credit course is a laboratory course, the TOTAL cost to him will be

    A. $504   B. $528   C. $542   D. $552

12.____

13. The graduating class of a certain community college consisted of 378 majors in secretarial science, 265 majors in engineering science, 57 majors in nursing, 513 majors in accounting, and 865 majors in liberal arts.
The percent of students who major in liberal arts at this college was MOST NEARLY

    A. 24.0%   B. 41.6%   C. 52.3%   D. 71.6%

13.____

14. Donald Smith earns $12.80 an hour for forty hours a week, with time and a half for all hours over forty. Last week, his total earnings amounted to $627.20.
He worked_____ hours.

    A. 46   B. 47   C. 48   D. 49

14.____

15. Mr. Jones desires to sell an article costing $28 at a gross profit of 30% of the selling price, and to allow a trade discount of 20% of the list price.
The list price of the article should be

    A. $43.68   B. $45.50   C. $48.00   D. $50.00

15.____

16. The gauge of an oil storage tank in an elementary school indicates 1/5 full. After a truck delivers 945 gallons of oil, the gauge indicates 4/5 full.
The capacity of the tank is _____ gallons.

    A. 1,260   B. 1,575   C. 1,625   D. 1,890

16.____

17. An invoice dated April 3, terms 3/10, 2/30, net/60, was paid in full with a check for $787.92 on May 1.
The amount of the invoice was

    A. $772.16   B. $787.92   C. $804.00   D. $812.29

17.____

18. Two pipes supply the water for the swimming pool at Blenheim High School. One pipe can fill the pool in 9 hours. The second pipe can fill the pool in 6 hours.
If both pipes were opened simultaneously, the pool could be filled in _____ hours minutes.

    A. 3; 36   B. 4; 30   C. 5; 15   D. 7; 30

18.____

19. John's father spent $24,000, which was one-fourth of his savings. He bought a car with three-eighths of the remainder of his savings.
His bank balance now amounts to

    A. $30,000   B. $32,000   C. $45,000   D. $50,000

19.____

20. A clock that loses 4 minutes every 24 hours was set at 6 A.M. on October 1.
    What time was indicated by the clock when the CORRECT time was 12:00 Noon on
    October 6th?
    _____ A.M.

    A. 11:36   B. 11:38   C. 11:39   D. 11:40

    20._____

21. Unit S's production fluctuated substantially from one year to another. In 2009, Unit S's
    production was 100% greater than in 2008. In 2010, production decreased by 25% from
    2009. In 2011, Unit S's production was 10% greater than in 2010. On the basis of this
    information, it is CORRECT to conclude that Unit S's production in 2011 exceeded Unit
    S's production in 2008 by

    A. 65%   B. 85%   C. 95%   D. 135%

    21._____

22. Agency X is moving into a new building. It has 1,500 employees presently on its staff and
    does not contemplate much variance from this level. The new building contains 100
    available offices, each with a maximum capacity of 30 employees. It has been decided
    that only 2/3 of the maximum capacity of each office will be utilized. The TOTAL number
    of offices that will be occupied by Agency X is

    A. 30   B. 66   C. 75   D. 90

    22._____

23. One typist completes a form letter every 5 minutes and another typist completes one
    every 6 minutes. If the two typists start together, how many minutes later will they again
    start typing new letters simultaneously and how many letters will they have completed by
    that time?
    _____ minutes - _____ letters.

    A. 11; 30   B. 12; 24   C. 24; 12   D. 30; 1

    23._____

24. During one week, a machine operator produces 10 fewer pages per hour of work than he
    usually does.
    If it ordinarily takes him six hours to produce a 300-page report, how many hours
    LONGER will that same 300-page report take him during the week when he produces
    more slowly?
    _____ hours longer.

    A. 1 1/2   B. 1 2/3   C. 2   D. 2 3/4

    24._____

25. A study reveals that Miss Brown files N cards in M hours, and Miss Smith files the same
    number of cards in T hours. If the two employees work together, the number of hours it
    will take them to file N cards is

    A. $\dfrac{N}{\dfrac{N}{M}+\dfrac{N}{N}}$

    B. $\dfrac{N}{T+M}+\dfrac{2N}{MT}$

    C. $N(\dfrac{M}{N}+\dfrac{N}{T})$

    D. $\dfrac{N}{NT+MN}$

    25._____

KEY (CORRECT ANSWERS)

1.	A	11.	B
2.	B	12.	B
3.	D	13.	B
4.	B	14.	A
5.	A	15.	D
6.	C	16.	B
7.	B	17.	C
8.	D	18.	A
9.	B	19.	C
10.	B	20.	C

21. A
22. C
23. D
24. A
25. A

SOLUTIONS TO PROBLEMS

1. 9/4 = 2 1/4" and 14/4 = 3 1/2"

2. Gross amount = (3)($6.75)(3.5) + (2)($6.75)(4.5) + ($8.00)(5.5) = $175.625, which is closest to selection B ($177.81).

3. $(529)(.35)(.89)(.67) \approx 110$

4. 10 worker-days are needed to type 125 letters, so (200)(10) ÷ 125 = 16 worker-days are needed to type 200 letters. Finally, 16 ÷ 10 workers = 1 3/5 days.

5. Index number = [(14)(10 1/2) + (3) (24) + (2) (12) + (1)(4 1/2) +

   (0)(5)] ÷ 56 ≈ 2.54

6. Typist X could do 30 forms in 30/20 = 1 1/2 hours. Let x = number of hours needed when working together with typist Y.

   Then, $(\dfrac{1}{1\frac{1}{2}})(x)+(\dfrac{1}{1})x=1$. Simplifying, 2x+3x=3, so $x=\dfrac{3}{5}$hr.= 36 min.

7. $(3+2+8+1+0+5) \div 6 = 3.\overline{16}$. Then, $18 \sim 3.\overline{6} = 14.8\overline{3}$.
   Finally, $14.8\overline{3} \div 18 \approx 82\%$

8. Wages = ($7.50)(40) + ($11.25)(8) = $390

9. (234)(15) = 3510 inside calls. Then, 5760 - 3510 = 2250 outside calls. Finally, 2250 - 2065 = 185 outside calls on the missing day.

10. 18 ÷ 3/4 = 24 feet long and 6 ÷ 3/4 = 8 feet wide.

11. Total weight = 1 lb. 11 oz. + 1 lb. 6 oz. + 2 lbs. 1 oz. + 2 lbs. 2 oz + 1 lb. 7 oz. +
    1 lb. 8 oz. + 6 oz. = 8 lbs. 41 oz. = 10 lbs. 9 oz.

12. Total cost = ($70)(7) + $24 + $14 = $528

13. 865 ÷ 2078 ≈ 41.6% liberal arts majors

14. ($12.80)(40)= $512, so he made $627.20 - $512 = $115.20 in overtime. His over-time rate = ($12.80)(1.5)= $19.20 per hour. Thus, he worked $115.20 ÷ $19.20 = 6 overtime hours. Total hours worked =46.

15. Let x = list price. Selling price = .80x. Then, .80x - (.30)(.80x) = $28. Simplifying, .56x = $28. Solving, x = $50.00

16. 945 gallons represents $\frac{4}{5} - \frac{1}{5} = \frac{3}{5}$ of the tank's capacity. Then, the capacity

    $= 945 \div \frac{3}{5} = 1575$ gallons

17. $787.92 \div .98 = $804.00

18. Let x = number of required hours. Then, (1/9)(x) + (1/6)(x) = 1 Simplifying, 2x + 3x = 18. Solving, x = 3.6 hours = 3 hrs. 36 min.

19. Bank balance = $96,000 - $24,000 - (3/8) ($72,000) = $45,000

20. From Oct. 1, 6 AM to Oct. 6, Noon = 5 1/2 days. The clock would show a loss of (4 min.)(5 1/2) = 21 min. Thus, the clock's time would (incorrectly) show 12:00 Noon - 21 min. = 11:39 AM

21. 2008 = x, 2009 = 200x, 2010 = 150x, 2011 = 165x
    65% more

22. (2/3)(30) = 20 employees in each office. Then, 1500 ÷ 20 = 75 offices

23. After 30 minutes, the typists will have finished a total of 6 + 5 = 11 letters.

24. When he works more slowly, he will only produce 300 - (6)(10) = 240 pages in 6 hrs. His new slower rate is 40 pages per hour, so he will need 60/40 = 1 1/2 more hours to do the remaining 60 pages.

25. Let x = required hours. Then, $(\frac{1}{M})(x)+(\frac{1}{T})(x)=1$. Simplifying, , x(T+M) = MT. Solving, x = MT/(T+M).
    Note: The N value is immaterial. Also, choice A reduces to MT/(T+M).

INTERPRETING STATISTICAL DATA
GRAPHS, CHARTS AND TABLES
TEST 1

DIRECTIONS: Each question or incomplete statement is followed by several suggested answers or completions. Select the one that BEST answers the question or completes the statement. *PRINT THE LETTER OF THE CORRECT ANSWER IN THE SPACE AT THE RIGHT.*

Questions 1-8.

DIRECTIONS: Questions 1 through 8 are to be answered SOLELY on the basis of the information and chart given below.

The following chart shows expenses in five selected categories for a one-year period expressed as percentages of these same expenses during the previous year. The chart compares two different offices. In Office T(represented by [   ]) a cost reduction program has oeen tested for the past year. The other office, Office Q(represented by [///////]) served as a control, in that no special effort was made to reduce costs during the past year.

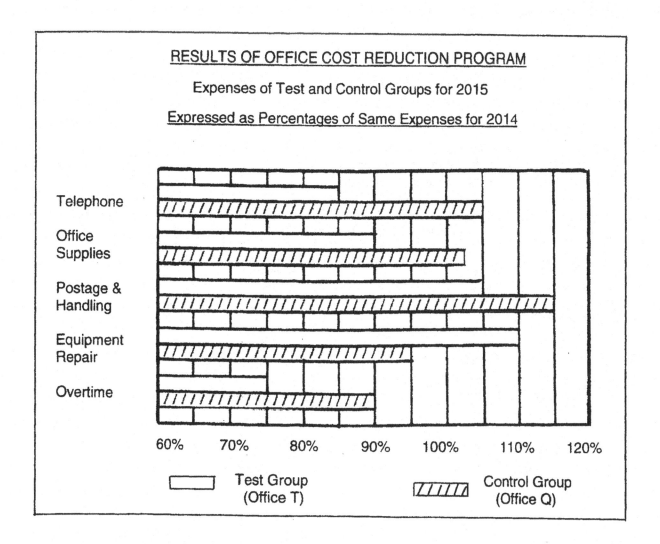

RESULTS OF OFFICE COST REDUCTION PROGRAM

Expenses of Test and Control Groups for 2015

Expressed as Percentages of Same Expenses for 2014

1. In Office T, which category of expense showed the GREATEST percentage reduction from 2014 to 2015?

    A. Telephone   B. Office supplies
    C. Postage and mailing   D. Overtime

    1.____

2. In which expense category did Office T show the BEST results in percentage terms when compared to Office Q?

    A. Telephone   B. Office supplies
    C. Postage and mailing   D. Overtime

    2.____

3. According to the above chart, the cost reduction program was LEAST effective for the expense category of

    A. Office supplies   B. Postage and mailing
    C. Equipment repair   D. Overtime

    3.____

4. Office T's telephone costs went down during 2015 by APPROXIMATELY how many percentage points?

    A. 15   B. 20   C. 85   D. 105

    4.____

5. Which of the following changes occurred in expenses for Office Supplies in Office Q in the year 2015 as compared with the year 2014?
They

    A. *increased* by more than 100%
    B. *remained* the same
    C. *decreased* by a few percentage points
    D. *increased* by a few percentage points

    5.____

6. For which of the following expense categories do the results in Office T and the results in Office Q differ MOST NEARLY by 10 percentage points?

    A. Telephone   B. Postage and mailing
    C. Equipment repair   D. Overtime

    6.____

7. In which expense category did Office Q's costs show the GREATEST percentage increase in 2015?

    A. Telephone   B. Office supplies
    C. Postage and mailing   D. Equipment repair

    7.____

8. In Office T, by APPROXIMATELY what percentage did overtime expense change during the past year?
It

    A. *increased* by 15%   B. *increased* by 75%
    C. *decreased* by 10%   D. *decreased* by 25%

    8.____

KEY (CORRECT ANSWERS)

1. D
2. A
3. C
4. A

5. D
6. B
7. C
8. D

———

TEST 2

Questions 1-7.

DIRECTIONS: Questions 1 through 7 are to be answered SOLELY on the basis of the information contained in the graph below which relates to the work of a public agency.

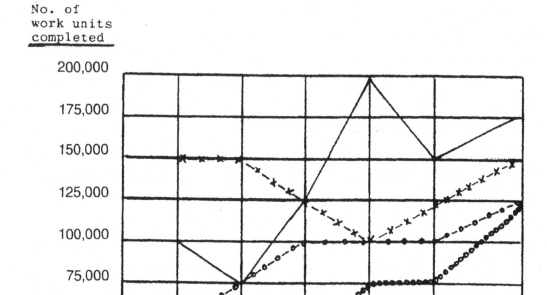

Units of each type of work completed by a public agency from 2011 to 2016

Letters Written ——————— Applications Processed 0—0—0—0

Documents Filed —x—x—x—x—x Inspections Made 0000000000000000

1. The year for which the number of units of one type of work completed was less than it was for the previous year while the number of each of the other types of work completed was more than it was for the previous year was

1.____

   A. 2012   B. 2013   C. 2014   D. 2015

2. The number of letters written exceeded the number of applications processed by the same amount in _____ of the years.

2.____

   A. two   B. three   C. four   D. five

3. The year in which the number of each type of work completed was GREATER than in the preceding year was   3.____

    A. 2013   B. 2014   C. 2015   D. 2016

4. The number of applications processed and the number of documents filed were the SAME in   4.____

    A. 2012   B. 2013   C. 2014   D. 2015

5. The TOTAL number of units of work completed by the agency   5.____

    A. increased in each year after 2011
    B. decreased from the prior year in two of the years after 2011
    C. was the same in two successive years from 2011 to 2016
    D. was less in 2011 than in any of the following years

6. For the year in which the number of letters written was twice as high as it was in 2011, the number of documents filed was _____ it was in 2011.   6.____

    A. the same as
    B. two-thirds of what
    C. five-sixths of what
    D. one and one-half times what

7. The variable which was the MOST stable during the period 2011 through 2016 was   7.____

    A. Inspections Made   B. Letters Written
    C. Documents Filed   D. Applications Processed

KEY (CORRECT ANSWERS)

1.	B		5.	C
2.	B		6.	B
3.	D		7.	D
4.	C			

TEST 3

Questions 1-10.

DIRECTIONS: Questions 1 through 10 are to be answered SOLELY on the basis of the REPORT OF TELEPHONE CALLS table given below.

TABLE – REPORT OF TELEPHONE CALLS

Dept.	No. of Sta-tions	No. of Employ-ees	No. of Incoming Calls In 2014	2015	No. of Long Distance Calls In 2014	2015	No. of Divisions
I	11	40	3421	4292	72	54	5
II	36	330	10392	10191	75	78	18
III	53	250	85243	85084	103	98	8
IV	24	60	9675	10123	82	85	6
V	13	30	5208	5492	54	48	6
VI	25	35	7472	8109	86	90	5
VII	37	195	11412	11299	68	72	11
VIII	36	54	8467	8674	59	68	4
IX	163	306	294321	289968	289	321	13
X	40	83	9588	8266	93	89	5
XI	24	68	7867	7433	86	87	13
XII	50	248	10039	10208	101	95	30
XIII	10	230	7550	6941	28	21	10
XIV	25	103	14281	14392	48	40	5
XV	19	230	8475	9206	38	43	8
XVI	22	45	4684	5584	39	48	10
XVII	41	58	10102	9677	49	52	6
XVIII	82	106	106242	105899	128	132	10
XIX	6	13	2649	2498	35	29	2
XX	16	30	1395	1468	78	90	2

1. The department which had more than 106,000 incoming calls in 2014 but fewer than 250,000 is

    A. II   B. IX   C. XVIII   D. III

1._____

2. The department which has fewer than 8 divisions and more than 100 but fewer than 300 employees is

    A. VII   B. XIV   C. XV   D. XVIII

2._____

3. The department which had an increase in 2015 over 2014 in the number of both incoming and long distance calls but had an increase in long distance calls of not more than 3

    A. IV   B. VI   C. XVII   D. XVIII

3._____

4. The department which had a decrease in the number of incoming calls in 2015 as compared to 2014 and has not less than 6 nor more than 7 divisions is

    A. IV   B. V   C. XVII   D. III

4._____

5. The department which has more than 7 divisions and more than 200 employees but fewer than 19 stations is

    A. XV   B. III   C. XX   D. XIII

5._____

6. The department having more than 10 divisions and fewer than 36 stations, which had an increase in long distance calls in 2015 over 2014, is

    A. XI   B. VII   C. XVI   D. XVIII

6._____

7. The department which in 2015 had at least 7,250 incoming calls and a decrease in long distance calls from 2014 and has more than 50 stations is   7.____

    A. IX   B. XII   C. XVIII   D. III

8. The department which has fewer than 25 stations, fewer than 100 employees, 10 or more divisions, and showed an increase of at least 9 long distance calls in 2015 over 2014 is   8.____

    A. IX   B. XVI   C. XX   D. XIII

9. The department which has more than 50 but fewer than 125 employees and had more than 5,000 incoming calls in 2014 but not more than 10,000, and more than 60 long distance calls in 2015 but not more than 85, and has more than 24 stations is   9.____

    A. VIII   B. XIV   C. IV   D. XI

10. If the number of departments showing an increase in long distance calls in 2015 over 1999 exceeds the number showing a decrease in long distance calls in the same period, select the Roman numeral indicating the department having less than one station for each 10 employees, provided not more than 8 divisions are served by that department. If the number of departments showing an increase in long distance calls in 2015 over 2014 does not exceed the number showing a decrease in long distance calls in the same period, select the Roman numeral indicating the department having the SMALLEST number of incoming calls in 2015.   10.____

    A. III   B. XIII   C. XV   D. XX

———

KEY (CORRECT ANSWERS)

1.	C	6.	A
2.	B	7.	D
3.	A	8.	B
4.	C	9.	A
5.	D	10.	C

———

TEST 4

Questions 1-6.

DIRECTIONS: Questions 1 through 6 are to be answered SOLELY on the basis of the information given in the chart below. This chart shows the results of a study made of the tasks performed by a stenographer during one day. Included in the chart are the time at which she started a certain task and, under the particular heading, the amount of time, in minutes, she took to complete the task, and explanations of telephone calls and miscellaneous activities. NOTE: The time spent at lunch should not be included in any of your calculations.

PAMELA JOB STUDY

NAME: Pamela Donald   DATE: 9/26
JOB TITLE: Stenographer
DIVISION: Stenographic Pool

Time of Start of Task	Taking Dicta-tion	Typ-ing	Fil-ing	Tele-phone Work	Hand-ling Mail	Misc. Acti-vities	Explanations of Telephone Calls and Miscellaneous Activities
9:00					22		
9:22						13	Picking up supplies
9:35						15	Cleaning typewriter
9:50	11						
10:01		30					
10:31				8			Call to Agency A
10:39	12						
10:51			10				
11:01				7			Call from Agency B
11:08		30					
11:38	10						
11:48				12			Call from Agency C
12:00	L	U	N	C	H		
1:00					28		
1:28	13						
1:41 2:13		32		12			Call to Agency B
X			15				
Y		50					
3:30	10						
3:40			21				
4:01				9			Call from Agency A
4:10	35						
4:45		9					
4:54						6	Cleaning up desk

SAMPLE QUESTION:

The total amount of time spent on miscellaneous activities in the morning is exactly equal to the total amount of time spent

     A. filing in the morning
     B. handling mail in the afternoon
     C. miscellaneous activities in the afternoon
     D. handling mail in the morning

Explanation of answer to sample question:

The total amount of time spent on miscellaneous activities in the morning equals 28 minutes (13 minutes for picking up supplies plus 15 minutes for cleaning the typewriter); and since it takes 28 minutes to handle mail in the afternoon, the answer is B.

1. The time labeled Y at which the stenographer started a typing assignment was   1._____

    A. 2:15   B. 2:25   C. 2:40   D. 2:50

2. The ratio of time spent on all incoming calls to time spent on all outgoing calls for the day was   2._____

    A. 5:7   B. 5:12   C. 7:5   D. 7:12

3. Of the following combinations of tasks, which ones take up exactly 80% of the total time spent on Tasks Performed during the day?   3._____

    A.   Typing, filing, telephone work, and handling mail
    B.   Taking dictation, filing, and miscellaneous activities
    C.   Taking dictation, typing, handling mail, and miscellaneous activities
    D.   Taking dictation, typing, filing, and telephone work

4. The total amount of time spent transcribing or typing work is how much MORE than the total amount of time spent in taking dictation?   4._____

    A. 55 minutes   B. 1 hour
    C. 1 hour 10 minutes   D. 1 hour 25 minutes

5. The GREATEST number of shifts in activities occurred between the times of   5._____

    A.   9:00 A.M. and 10:31 A.M.
    B.   9:35 A.M. and 11:01 A.M.
    C.   10:31 A.M. and 12:00 Noon
    D.   3:30 P.M. and 5:00 P.M.

6. The total amount of time spent on taking dictation in the morning plus the total amount of time spent on filing in the afternoon is exactly EQUAL to the total amount of time spent on   6._____

    A.   typing in the afternoon minus the total amount of time spent on telephone work in the afternoon
    B.   typing in the morning plus the total amount of time spent on miscellaneous activities in the afternoon
    C.   dictation in the afternoon plus the total amount of time spent on filing in the morning
    D.   typing in the afternoon minus the total amount of time spent on handling mail in the morning

---

KEY (CORRECT ANSWERS)

1.	C	4.	B
2.	C	5.	C
3.	D	6.	D

TEST 5

Questions 1-8.

DIRECTIONS: Questions 1 through 8 are to be answered SOLELY on the basis of the information given in the table below.

	Bronx		Brooklyn		Manhattan		Queens		Richmond	
	May	June	May	June	May	June	May	June	May	June
Number of Clerks in Office Assigned To Issue Applications for Licenses	3	4	6	8	6	8	3	5	3	4
Number of Licenses Issued	950	1010	1620	1940	1705	2025	895	1250	685	975
Amount Collected in License Fees	$42,400	$52,100	$77,600	$94,500	$83,700	$98,800	$39,300	$65,500	$30,600	$48,200
Number of Inspectors	4	5	6	7	7	8	4	5	2	4
Number of Inspections Made	420	450	630	710	690	740	400	580	320	440
Number of Violations Found as a Result of Inspections	211	153	352	378	320	385	256	304	105	247

1. Of the following statements, the one which is NOT accurate on the basis of an inspection of the information contained in the table is that, for each office, the increase from May to June in the number of

    1.____

    A. inspectors was accompanied by an increase in the number of inspections made
    B. licenses issued was accompanied by an increase in the amount collected in license fees
    C. inspections made was accompanied by an increase in the number of violations found
    D. licenses issued was accompanied by an increase in the number of clerks assigned to issue applications for licenses

2. The TOTAL number of licenses issued by all five offices in the Division in May was

    2.____

    A. 4800   B. 5855   C. 6865   D. 7200

3. The total number of inspectors in all five borough offices in June exceeded the number in   3._____
May by MOST NEARLY

    A. 21%   B. 26%   C. 55%   D. 70%

4. In the month of June, the number of violations found per inspection made was the HIGH-   4._____
EST in

    A. Brooklyn   B. Manhattan   C. Queens   D. Richmond

5. In the month of May, the average number of inspections made by an inspector in the   5._____
Bronx was the same as the average number of inspections made by an inspector in

    A. Brooklyn   B. Manhattan   C. Queens   D. Richmond

6. Assume that in June all of the inspectors in the Division spent 7 hours a day making   6._____
inspections on each of the 21 working days in the month.
Then the average amount of time that an inspector in the Manhattan office spent on an
inspection that month was MOST NEARLY

    A. 2 hours   B. 1 hour and 35 minutes
    C. 1 hour and 3 minutes   D. 38 minutes

7. If an average fine of $100 was imposed for a violation found by the Division, what was the   7._____
TOTAL amount in fines imposed for all the violations found by the Division in May?

    A. $124,400   B. $133,500   C. $146,700   D. $267,000

8. Assume that the amount collected in license fees by the entire Division in May was 80   8._____
percent of the amount collected by the entire Division in April.
How much was collected by the entire Division in April?

    A. $218,880   B. $328,320   C. $342,000   D. $410,400

KEY (CORRECT ANSWERS)

1.	C	5.	A
2.	B	6.	B
3.	B	7.	A
4.	D	8.	C

TEST 6

Questions 1-8.

DIRECTIONS: Questions 1 through 8 are to be answered SOLELY on the basis of the information contained in the chart and table shown below, which relate to Bureau X in a certain public agency. The chart shows the percentage of the bureau's annual expenditures spent on equipment, supplies, and salaries for each of the years 2012-2016. The table shows the bureau's annual expenditures for each of the years 2012-2016.

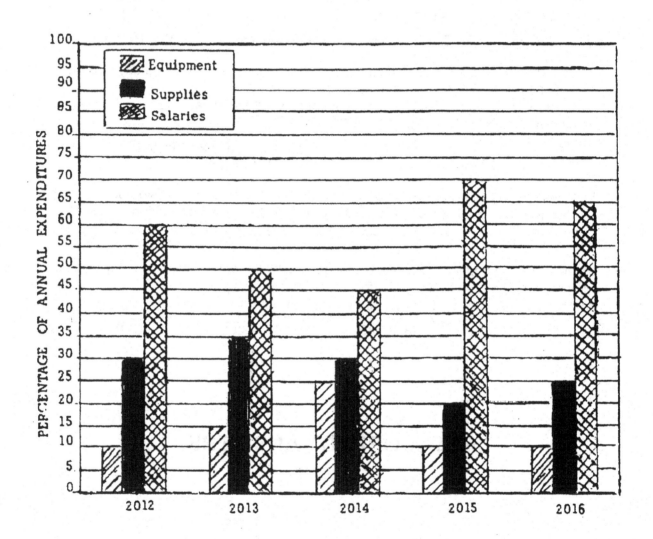

The bureau's annual expenditures for the years 2012-2016 are shown in the following table:

YEAR	EXPENDITURES
2012	$ 8,000,000
2013	$12,000,000
2014	$15,000,000
2015	$10,000,000
2016	$12,000,000

Equipment, supplies, and salaries were the only three categories for which the bureau spent money.

Candidates may find it useful to arrange their computations on their scratch paper in an orderly manner since the correct computations for one question may also be helpful in answering another question.

1. The information contained in the chart and table is sufficient to determine the   1._____

   A. average annual salary of an employee in the bureau in 2013
   B. decrease in the amount of money spent on supplies in the bureau in 2012 from the amount spent in the preceding year
   C. changes between 2014 and 2015 in the prices of supplies bought by the bureau
   D. increase in the amount of money spent on salaries in the bureau in 2016 over the amount spent in the preceding year

2. If the percentage of expenditures for salaries in one year is added to the percentage of   2._____
   expenditures for equipment in that year, a total of two percentages for that year is obtained.
   The two years for which this total is the SAME are

   A. 2012 and 2014   B. 2013 and 2015
   C. 2012 and 2015   D. 2013 and 2016

3. Of the following, the year in which the bureau spent the GREATEST amount of money on   3._____
   supplies was

   A. 2016   B. 2014   C. 2008   D. 2012

4. Of the following years, the one in which there was the GREATEST increase over the pre-   4._____
   ceding year in the amount of money spent on salaries is

   A. 2015   B. 2016   C. 2013   D. 2014

5. Of the bureau's expenditures for equipment in 2016, one-third was used for the purchase   5._____
   of mailroom equipment and the remainder was spent on miscellaneous office equipment.
   How much did the bureau spend on miscellaneous office equipment in 2016?

   A. $4,000,000   B. $400,000
   C. $8,000,000   D. $800,000

6. If there were 120 employees in the bureau in 2015, then the average annual salary paid   6._____
   to the employees in that year was MOST NEARLY

   A. $43,450   B. $49,600   C. $58,350   D. $80,800

7. In 2014, the bureau had 125 employees.   7._____
   If 20 of the employees earned an average annual salary of $80,000, then the average
   salary of the other 105 employees was MOST NEARLY

   A. $49,000   B. $64,000   C. $41,000   D. $54,000

8. Assume that the bureau estimated that the amount of money it would spend on supplies in 2017 would be the same as the amount it spent on that category in 2016. Similarly, the bureau estimated that the amount of money it would spend on equipment in 2017 would be the same as the amount it spent on that category in 2016. However, the bureau estimated that in 2017 the amount it would spend on salaries would be 10 percent higher than the amount it spent on that category in 2016.
The percentage of its annual expenditures that the bureau estimated it would spend on supplies in 2017 is MOST NEARLY

    A. 27.5%   B. 23.5%   C. 22.5%   D. 25%

8.____

KEY (CORRECT ANSWERS)

1.	D	5.	D
2.	A	6.	C
3.	B	7.	A
4.	C	8.	B
